MARL for Next-Generation AI

Harnessing Multi-Agent Reinforcement Learning to
Build Smarter, Autonomous AI Systems

James Acklin

Copyright Page

Table of Contents

1. Introduction to Multi-Agent Reinforcement Learning

The Rise of Multi-Agent Reinforcement Learning in AI

Artificial intelligence has made significant progress in recent years, with reinforcement learning (RL) playing a crucial role in developing systems that learn through interaction with their environment. Traditional RL focuses on a **single agent**, which learns by taking actions and receiving feedback in the form of rewards. However, many real-world problems involve multiple decision-making entities that interact with each other, often pursuing different or even conflicting goals. This has led to the development of **Multi-Agent Reinforcement Learning (MARL)**, an extension of RL that enables multiple intelligent agents to operate in shared environments.

MARL is not a new concept, but its importance has increased due to advancements in computational power, the availability of large-scale training environments, and the growing demand for AI-driven automation. It has become a critical area of research and application in robotics, finance, autonomous systems, and strategic decision-making. The complexity of interactions in multi-agent environments makes MARL a challenging but necessary step toward developing AI systems that can handle dynamic, real-world scenarios.

A key factor behind the growth of MARL is the increasing need for **coordination, competition, and collaboration** among AI agents. Unlike traditional RL, where an agent learns by interacting with a static environment, MARL introduces an additional layer of complexity. Each agent's actions affect not only its own learning process but also the experiences of other agents in the same environment. This makes the learning process more dynamic and introduces unique challenges such as **non-stationarity**, where the environment constantly changes as agents update their strategies.

Recent advances in deep learning have provided the foundation for scaling MARL to complex problems. Techniques such as **Deep Q-Networks (DQN),**

Proximal Policy Optimization (PPO), and Multi-Agent Deep Deterministic Policy Gradient (MADDPG) have allowed agents to process high-dimensional inputs and learn sophisticated policies. These methods have enabled AI systems to operate in increasingly complex multi-agent settings, including large-scale simulations and real-world applications.

The rise of MARL is closely tied to its practical applications. In **autonomous driving**, for example, self-driving cars must interact with other vehicles, pedestrians, and traffic systems. Each decision a car makes affects the safety and efficiency of the entire system. MARL allows autonomous vehicles to learn cooperative behaviors, such as merging into traffic safely or responding to unexpected road conditions.

Similarly, in **robotics and industrial automation**, multiple robots must coordinate to complete tasks efficiently. Warehouses operated by fleets of robots use MARL to optimize movement, minimize collisions, and ensure smooth operations. These AI-driven systems adapt to changing workloads and environments, making them more reliable and efficient than traditional rule-based automation.

Competitive environments also benefit from MARL. In **finance**, trading algorithms interact with one another, constantly adjusting their strategies based on market conditions. MARL enables trading bots to optimize their decision-making by learning from past trades and anticipating the actions of competing algorithms. This ability to adapt to a dynamic financial landscape has led to more sophisticated trading strategies and risk management techniques.

Another area where MARL has made a significant impact is **AI-driven gaming**. Systems like DeepMind's **AlphaStar**, which achieved grandmaster-level performance in the real-time strategy game StarCraft II, demonstrate the effectiveness of MARL in competitive settings. In these environments, multiple AI agents must make strategic decisions while anticipating and responding to their opponents' actions. Unlike traditional board games such as chess, where moves are sequential, these games require AI to process simultaneous interactions, making MARL a necessary approach.

As MARL continues to advance, researchers are addressing its challenges, including **scalability, stability, and efficient training methods**. The field is evolving rapidly, with new techniques improving how agents communicate, cooperate, and make decisions in uncertain environments. The expansion of MARL into real-world applications marks an important shift in AI, moving beyond isolated intelligence toward systems capable of working together in complex, unpredictable settings.

The development of MARL reflects a broader trend in artificial intelligence: the transition from **individual AI agents to interconnected, adaptive multi-agent systems**. As industries increasingly rely on AI for automation, decision-making, and optimization, MARL will play an essential role in shaping the next generation of intelligent systems.

Key Concepts and Motivation

Multi-Agent Reinforcement Learning (MARL) builds upon the foundation of **Reinforcement Learning (RL)**, a machine learning technique where an **agent** learns by interacting with an **environment** and receiving **rewards** or **penalties** based on its actions. The goal of the agent is to maximize its cumulative reward over time.

In MARL, multiple agents operate in the same environment, each making decisions that influence not only their own outcomes but also the experiences of other agents. These agents may **cooperate**, **compete**, or act **independently**, depending on the nature of the environment and their objectives.

MARL introduces several key concepts that distinguish it from single-agent RL. Understanding these concepts is essential for designing and training multi-agent systems effectively.

Key Concepts in MARL

1. Multi-Agent Environment

A **multi-agent environment** is a setting where multiple AI agents interact, either directly or indirectly. Unlike single-agent RL, where the environment remains static except for the actions of one agent, a multi-agent environment is dynamic because every agent's actions influence the conditions in which other agents operate.

These environments can be **fully observable** (where all agents have access to complete information) or **partially observable** (where each agent has limited knowledge of the system). The level of observability affects how agents learn and coordinate their actions.

2. Types of Multi-Agent Interactions

The way agents interact determines their learning strategies and objectives. MARL environments typically fall into three main categories:

Cooperative: Agents share a common goal and work together to maximize a shared reward. Examples include robotic teams performing a task or self-driving cars coordinating to reduce traffic congestion.

Competitive: Agents have conflicting goals, and one agent's success may lead to another's failure. Examples include AI-driven stock trading systems or AI opponents in strategy games.

Mixed: Some agents cooperate while others compete. This is common in real-world settings such as online marketplaces, where companies compete for customers while also relying on shared infrastructure.

3. Non-Stationarity in MARL

Non-stationarity is a fundamental challenge in MARL. In single-agent RL, the environment is considered fixed, meaning the agent's learning process remains stable. However, in MARL, every agent **continuously updates its strategy**, causing the environment to change dynamically. This means that what was once an optimal strategy may no longer be effective as other agents adapt.

Because of non-stationarity, traditional RL methods struggle in multi-agent settings. MARL requires specialized techniques to handle these shifting conditions, such as training agents in **simulated environments** or using **centralized training with decentralized execution (CTDE)**.

4. Credit Assignment Problem

In cooperative environments, multiple agents contribute to achieving a shared objective. The **credit assignment problem** refers to the difficulty of determining which agent's actions led to success or failure. Since rewards are often distributed among all agents, it can be unclear whether an individual agent made a positive contribution or simply benefited from the efforts of others.

To address this, researchers use techniques like **reward shaping**, where agents receive intermediate rewards that reflect their specific contributions, or **counterfactual credit assignment**, which compares an agent's impact to what would have happened had it taken a different action.

5. Coordination and Communication

In many multi-agent systems, agents must **exchange information** to make better decisions. This is especially true in cooperative environments where teamwork is essential. Some MARL approaches allow agents to develop **emergent communication**, meaning they learn to share meaningful signals even without predefined rules.

Coordination strategies vary based on how much information agents are allowed to share. Some systems use **centralized learning**, where all agents have access to a shared training process, while others rely on **decentralized learning**, where each agent learns independently based on its observations.

Motivation for MARL

The development of MARL is driven by the need to create **AI systems that can handle environments with multiple decision-makers**. Many real-world scenarios involve **interacting entities** that must learn, adapt, and optimize their behavior. Traditional single-agent RL is not sufficient for these tasks, making MARL a necessary extension.

Several factors contribute to the growing interest in MARL:

1. Real-World Complexity Requires Multi-Agent Decision-Making

Many real-world problems involve **multiple independent agents** operating in the same space. Autonomous vehicles, for example, do not function in isolation. They must interact with other vehicles, pedestrians, and infrastructure. A single-agent RL approach would not be effective in handling the complexity of **traffic systems**, where cooperation and competition occur simultaneously.

Similarly, modern supply chains involve numerous AI-driven systems, including **robotic warehouses, transportation networks, and inventory management systems**. These systems must work together efficiently to optimize delivery times and reduce costs. MARL provides the framework for developing AI models that can **coordinate and optimize** multi-agent operations.

2. Advances in Computational Power Enable Large-Scale MARL

Training multiple agents simultaneously requires significant computing resources. In the past, limited processing power made large-scale MARL impractical. However, recent improvements in **GPU acceleration, cloud computing, and parallel processing** have made it possible to train and test MARL models at scale.

The availability of **high-quality simulation environments** has also contributed to MARL's progress. Platforms like **PettingZoo, OpenAI Gym, and StarCraft II Learning Environment** provide robust testbeds for training and evaluating multi-agent systems.

3. The Need for AI Systems That Adapt to Dynamic Environments

Traditional AI models are often designed for **static, rule-based environments**, meaning they struggle when faced with unpredictable interactions. Many industries require AI solutions that can **adapt in real time**.

In finance, for example, algorithmic trading systems must adjust their strategies based on the behavior of competing AI traders. In cybersecurity, AI-driven defense systems must **react dynamically** to evolving cyber threats. MARL provides the ability to build AI models that continuously refine their behavior based on changing conditions.

4. The Push for General AI and Emergent Intelligence

A long-term goal of artificial intelligence research is to develop **general intelligence**, where AI systems can operate flexibly across different domains. MARL moves AI closer to this goal by enabling systems that **learn collectively, make decentralized decisions, and adapt to new environments**.

Emergent intelligence—where complex behaviors arise from simple interactions—is a significant motivation for MARL research. Just as biological systems exhibit complex group behavior through simple local rules, MARL agents can learn to form strategies without being explicitly programmed for every possible scenario. This has significant implications for AI-driven robotics, where teams of simple agents can work together to accomplish complex tasks.

MARL introduces new challenges and opportunities in artificial intelligence. By enabling AI agents to learn **collaboratively or competitively** in dynamic environments, MARL makes it possible to develop intelligent systems that go beyond single-agent learning. The increasing complexity of real-world applications, coupled with advancements in computational power, has made MARL a growing area of research and innovation.

The ability of MARL to handle **multi-agent interactions, adapt to changing conditions, and scale to large environments** makes it a critical step toward creating intelligent, autonomous systems capable of operating in complex domains. As AI continues to evolve, MARL will play a central role in shaping the future of intelligent automation, robotics, and decision-making systems.

Applications in Real-World Systems

Multi-Agent Reinforcement Learning (MARL) is being used in various industries where multiple AI-driven decision-makers must interact. Unlike traditional single-agent reinforcement learning, where one agent learns by interacting with a static environment, MARL enables multiple agents to operate simultaneously, making decisions that impact both their outcomes and the outcomes of others. This capability allows MARL to be applied in dynamic, interactive environments where coordination, competition, and adaptability are essential.

Many industries are now integrating MARL to solve complex challenges that involve multiple interacting entities. These applications range from **autonomous transportation systems** to **finance, robotics, gaming, and smart infrastructure**.

Autonomous Vehicles and Smart Transportation

One of the most practical uses of MARL is in **autonomous driving**. Self-driving cars do not operate in isolation; they must interact with other vehicles, traffic signals, pedestrians, and changing road conditions. Each vehicle acts as an **intelligent agent** that must make real-time decisions while considering the actions of others.

MARL allows autonomous vehicles to:

Coordinate lane merging and overtaking maneuvers. A self-driving car must predict how surrounding vehicles will react to its movements and adjust its speed accordingly. MARL helps agents learn strategies that optimize both **efficiency and safety**.

Adapt to traffic conditions dynamically. In urban environments, traffic flow is constantly changing. MARL enables AI agents to **adjust routes, optimize traffic signals, and reduce congestion** by learning from real-time conditions.

Improve accident avoidance. Traditional rule-based driving models cannot handle unexpected behaviors from human drivers or road hazards. MARL helps autonomous vehicles anticipate risks and take **proactive safety measures**.

By integrating MARL into transportation systems, traffic efficiency can be improved, leading to reduced travel time, lower fuel consumption, and enhanced road safety.

Robotics and Industrial Automation

Many industries rely on robots to perform repetitive or hazardous tasks. In **industrial automation**, MARL helps robots work together more efficiently, reducing costs and increasing productivity. Unlike traditional automation, where robots follow **pre-programmed instructions**, MARL allows robots to **adapt their behavior** based on real-time conditions and interactions with other robots.

Some of the key uses in robotics and automation include:

Warehouse management and logistics. Companies like Amazon and DHL use **autonomous warehouse robots** to transport packages efficiently. MARL allows these robots to coordinate movements, prevent congestion, and optimize delivery paths.

Collaborative assembly lines. In manufacturing, multiple robotic arms and conveyor systems must work together to assemble products. MARL helps these systems coordinate their movements to **minimize errors and maximize efficiency**.

Search and rescue missions. In emergency situations, MARL can be used in **autonomous drones** that search disaster zones for survivors. Each drone acts as an independent agent, but they share information and adjust their search patterns based on real-time data.

MARL enhances robotic collaboration by making autonomous systems more **flexible and adaptive**, allowing them to handle complex tasks that require continuous decision-making.

Financial Markets and Algorithmic Trading

In financial markets, multiple traders, institutions, and automated systems interact to buy and sell assets. MARL is used in **algorithmic trading**, where AI agents make trading decisions based on market conditions. Unlike traditional trading models, which rely on predefined rules, MARL-based agents continuously learn and adjust their strategies based on market fluctuations and the behavior of other traders.

MARL is applied in finance to:

Optimize trading strategies. Trading algorithms use MARL to analyze market trends and adjust their trading decisions based on the actions of competing traders.

Enhance risk management. In volatile markets, MARL helps AI-driven financial models predict potential losses and adjust investments to minimize risks.

Detect fraudulent transactions. Financial fraud detection systems use MARL to **identify patterns of suspicious behavior** by analyzing multiple interacting entities, such as buyers, sellers, and transaction networks.

By integrating MARL into trading and financial analysis, institutions can make **faster, more informed decisions** while reducing risks associated with market fluctuations.

Healthcare and Medical AI

Healthcare systems involve **multiple decision-makers**, including doctors, nurses, pharmacists, and administrative staff. AI-driven healthcare systems require multi-agent coordination to improve **diagnosis, treatment planning, and hospital management**. MARL is being used to improve healthcare efficiency by optimizing resource allocation, patient treatment, and emergency response strategies.

Some key applications in healthcare include:

AI-driven diagnostics. MARL is used to train **collaborative diagnostic systems**, where multiple AI models analyze different aspects of a patient's condition and work together to improve diagnostic accuracy.

Optimizing hospital resources. In large medical facilities, AI agents help **allocate staff, schedule surgeries, and manage patient flow** to ensure efficient use of resources.

Personalized treatment planning. AI models use MARL to adjust treatment strategies based on how patients respond to previous treatments. By integrating real-time feedback, AI-driven treatment plans can be continuously improved.

MARL in healthcare has the potential to **reduce costs, improve patient outcomes, and enhance hospital efficiency** by enabling AI agents to work together in complex, decision-driven environments.

Gaming and AI Strategy Development

MARL is widely used in **game development and AI competition**. In video games, AI agents need to **react to player decisions, coordinate team strategies, and adapt to changing environments**. Multiplayer games require AI systems that can **compete against human players or collaborate in team-based scenarios**.

Notable applications include:

Game AI for strategy games. DeepMind's **AlphaStar**, which achieved **grandmaster-level performance in StarCraft II**, used MARL to train AI agents that adapt to human strategies and optimize their actions in real-time.

Adaptive difficulty in gaming. Modern AI-driven games use MARL to **adjust difficulty levels based on player behavior**, ensuring a more engaging experience.

AI for real-time multiplayer cooperation. Games like Dota 2 and League of Legends require AI teammates that **coordinate with human players** and make strategic decisions in a dynamic environment.

Gaming provides an ideal testing environment for MARL research, as it allows developers to experiment with **multi-agent coordination, competition, and adaptation** in controlled settings.

Smart Infrastructure and Energy Systems

MARL is also transforming the way **smart cities and energy systems** are managed. In smart infrastructure, multiple agents must **work together to optimize energy use, traffic flow, and resource distribution**.

Examples of MARL applications in smart infrastructure include:

Smart grid optimization. Electricity grids rely on MARL to **balance supply and demand** across multiple power stations, reducing energy waste and improving efficiency.

Autonomous traffic signal control. AI-driven traffic systems use MARL to **adjust traffic lights based on real-time congestion data**, improving urban mobility.

Disaster response and infrastructure management. AI agents help predict and respond to disasters by analyzing data from multiple sources, such as sensors, weather reports, and emergency services.

By integrating MARL into infrastructure systems, cities can **become more efficient, reduce operational costs, and improve quality of life** for residents.

MARL is being applied in industries that require multiple AI-driven decision-makers to interact, adapt, and optimize their behavior. From **self-driving cars and financial markets to healthcare, robotics, gaming, and smart**

infrastructure, MARL enables AI agents to **collaborate, compete, and make decisions in real-time**.

As research in MARL advances, its impact will continue to grow, leading to **more intelligent, adaptive, and scalable AI systems** across industries. The ability to train multiple agents to **learn, cooperate, and respond dynamically** is paving the way for more efficient automation, improved decision-making, and greater innovation in AI-driven applications.

2. Fundamentals of Reinforcement Learning

Reinforcement Learning (RL) is a core component of artificial intelligence that allows systems to **learn from experience** rather than relying on predefined rules. Instead of following a fixed set of instructions, an RL agent interacts with an environment, takes actions, and **learns from the feedback it receives**. This learning process is what enables RL-based AI systems to improve their decision-making over time.

To fully understand **Multi-Agent Reinforcement Learning (MARL)**, it's essential to grasp the **fundamental principles of RL** first. In this chapter, we will explore the **core mathematical framework** behind RL, explain different learning approaches, and introduce key algorithms that serve as building blocks for MARL.

Markov Decision Processes and Partially Observable MDPs

Reinforcement learning is all about decision-making in uncertain environments, and at the core of this field is the **Markov Decision Process (MDP)**. This mathematical framework helps us describe **how an agent interacts with its environment**, how it makes decisions based on its observations, and how it learns from rewards.

A single-agent reinforcement learning problem almost always starts with defining it as an MDP. This structure allows us to model **sequential decision-making**, where each action the agent takes influences future states. However, in many real-world situations, an agent does not have full knowledge of the environment, leading to what we call a **Partially Observable Markov Decision Process (POMDP)**.

Markov Decision Processes (MDPs)

An **MDP** is a mathematical model that describes an **agent's interaction with an environment** over time. It consists of a set of states, a set of possible actions, a transition model that describes how the environment changes in response to an agent's actions, and a reward function that guides the agent's behavior.

Formally, an MDP is defined as a **5-tuple**:

$(S,A,P,R,\gamma)(S, A, P, R, \gamma)$

where:

SS is the set of possible states in the environment.

AA is the set of actions available to the agent.

P(s'|s,a)P(s' | s, a) is the transition function that defines the probability of reaching state **s's'** given that the agent was in state **ss** and took action **aa**.

R(s,a)R(s, a) is the reward function that assigns a numerical reward when the agent takes action **aa** in state **ss**.

γ**gamma** (gamma) is the discount factor, which determines the importance of future rewards compared to immediate rewards.

Breaking Down the MDP Components

When an agent interacts with an MDP environment, it follows a loop:

The agent **observes** the current state **ss**.

The agent **chooses an action aa** based on a policy.

The environment **transitions** to a new state **s's'** based on the probability distribution **P(s'|s,a)P(s' | s, a)**.

The agent **receives a reward** based on **R(s,a)R(s, a)**.

This process **repeats** until the agent reaches a terminal state.

An important feature of MDPs is that they satisfy the **Markov property**, which means that the next state depends **only** on the current state and action, not on past states. This property simplifies learning because it ensures that an agent doesn't need to remember the entire history of its interactions—only the current state matters.

A Simple Real-World Example: Robot Navigation

To make this more concrete, let's consider a **robot navigating a grid-based environment**. The robot can move **up, down, left, or right**, and it receives a reward when it reaches a goal location.

MDP Representation of the Robot Navigation Problem

States: The position of the robot on the grid (e.g., **(x, y) coordinates**).

Actions: Moving **up, down, left, or right**.

Transition Function: If the robot moves right from (2,2), it may end up at (3,2) with probability **0.9** but might slip and end up at (2,3) with probability **0.1**.

Rewards: A **+10 reward** for reaching the goal, **-1 penalty** for hitting a wall, and **0 otherwise**.

Discount Factor (γ\gamma): Determines how much the agent values future rewards. A lower gamma means the agent prefers immediate rewards, while a higher gamma encourages long-term planning.

Implementing an MDP in Python

We can simulate an MDP using Python. Let's create a simple **grid-based environment** for an agent to navigate.

```python
import numpy as np

class GridWorld:
    def __init__(self, size=4, goal=(3, 3),
penalty=-1, gamma=0.9):
        self.size = size
        self.goal = goal
        self.penalty = penalty
        self.gamma = gamma
        self.state = (0, 0)  # Start position

    def step(self, action):
        x, y = self.state
        if action == "up":
            x = max(0, x - 1)
        elif action == "down":
            x = min(self.size - 1, x + 1)
```

```
        elif action == "left":
            y = max(0, y - 1)
        elif action == "right":
            y = min(self.size - 1, y + 1)

        self.state = (x, y)

        if self.state == self.goal:
            return self.state, 10, True   # Goal
reached
        else:
            return self.state, self.penalty, False
# Keep going

# Example usage
env = GridWorld()
state, reward, done = env.step("right")
print(f"New State: {state}, Reward: {reward}, Done:
{done}")
```

In this simple **GridWorld MDP**, the agent moves according to actions, receives rewards, and transitions between states. This structure mirrors **real-world navigation problems** where autonomous robots must make movement decisions under uncertainty.

Partially Observable Markov Decision Processes (POMDPs)

In many real-world situations, an agent **does not have complete knowledge of the state**. For example, a self-driving car cannot "see" the entire traffic system—it only receives sensor readings from its immediate surroundings. This is where **Partially Observable Markov Decision Processes (POMDPs)** come into play.

A **POMDP** extends an MDP by introducing **observations**. Instead of directly seeing the environment's full state, the agent receives **partial observations**, which it must use to infer the actual state.

A POMDP is defined as a **7-tuple**:

$(S, A, P, R, O, Z, \gamma)$

where:

OO is the set of possible **observations** the agent can receive.

$Z(o|s',a)$Z(o | s', a) is the **observation function**, defining the probability of observing oo given that the new state is s's' after taking action aa.

Example: Self-Driving Car (POMDP Application)

A self-driving car operates under **partial observability** because its sensors provide **limited** and **noisy** data about the road, pedestrians, and obstacles. The actual state of traffic is unknown, and the car must **infer the environment** based on sensor readings.

For example:

States: Traffic conditions at intersections.

Actions: Accelerate, brake, turn left, turn right.

Observations: Sensor readings (pedestrian detection, speed of surrounding cars).

Observation Function: The likelihood of seeing a pedestrian based on sensor noise.

Markov Decision Processes (MDPs) provide a foundation for reinforcement learning, allowing agents to make **sequential decisions** in structured environments. However, when an agent does not have full knowledge of the environment, a Partially Observable Markov Decision Process (POMDP) is needed to model **uncertainty**.

The concepts of MDPs and POMDPs are widely used in **robotics, autonomous systems, healthcare, and finance**, where decision-making under uncertainty is crucial. Understanding these principles is essential for developing intelligent, adaptive AI systems that can handle **real-world unpredictability**.

Value-Based and Policy-Based Learning

Reinforcement Learning (RL) provides a framework for **decision-making in uncertain environments**, where an agent learns by interacting with an environment and receiving rewards for its actions. The goal is to find an optimal strategy that maximizes cumulative rewards over time.

There are two primary approaches to reinforcement learning: **value-based learning** and **policy-based learning**. These methods define how an agent determines the best action to take in any given situation. Understanding these approaches is essential for building intelligent systems that can learn and adapt to dynamic environments.

This discussion will provide a clear, structured explanation of both methods, their strengths and limitations, and how they apply to real-world problems.

Value-Based Learning

Value-based learning is a reinforcement learning approach where an agent learns to estimate the **value** of being in a particular state or taking a specific action. The agent then selects actions that maximize this value, ensuring that it achieves the highest possible long-term reward.

How Value-Based Learning Works

In value-based learning, the agent maintains a function that assigns a numerical score, known as a **value**, to states or state-action pairs. This value represents the expected total reward the agent can obtain from that state or action onward.

There are two main types of value functions:

State-Value Function ($V(s)V(s)$): Represents the expected total reward the agent will receive if it starts in state **ss** and follows an optimal strategy.

Action-Value Function ($Q(s,a)Q(s, a)$): Represents the expected total reward the agent will receive if it takes action **aa** in state **ss** and then follows an optimal strategy.

The **Bellman Equation**, a fundamental principle in RL, describes how these values are updated based on experience:

$Q(s,a)=R(s,a)+\gamma\max_{a'}Q(s',a')$ Q(s, a) = R(s, a) + \gamma \max_{a'} Q(s', a')

where:

$Q(s,a)$ Q(s, a) is the value of taking action aa in state ss.

$R(s,a)$ R(s, a) is the immediate reward received.

γ\gamma (gamma) is the discount factor, which determines the importance of future rewards.

s's' is the next state reached after taking action aa.

$\max_{a'}Q(s',a')$\max_{a'} Q(s', a') represents the maximum value of the next possible actions.

The agent **learns the Q-values iteratively** by exploring the environment, storing experiences, and updating estimates using the Bellman equation.

Example: Robot Navigation

Consider a simple **robot navigating a warehouse**. The robot receives rewards for reaching designated zones and penalties for hitting obstacles. Using value-based learning, it assigns values to different positions and movement actions, learning to **choose paths that maximize efficiency and avoid obstacles**.

For example:

If the robot is at **position A**, moving to **position B** might have a higher Q-value because it leads to an efficient route.

If an obstacle is in a certain direction, the Q-value of moving toward it will be lower, discouraging the agent from choosing that action.

Q-Learning: A Popular Value-Based Algorithm

Q-learning is one of the most widely used **value-based RL algorithms**. It is an **off-policy** method, meaning the agent learns from previously collected experiences rather than relying only on current interactions.

A simple Python implementation of **Q-learning** for a small grid environment is shown below:

```python
import numpy as np

# Define environment parameters
num_states = 5   # Number of states
num_actions = 2   # Number of possible actions
Q_table = np.zeros((num_states, num_actions))   #
Initialize Q-table with zeros
learning_rate = 0.1   # Step size for updates
discount_factor = 0.9   # Future reward discount
epsilon = 0.1   # Exploration rate

# Sample reward function
reward_matrix = np.array([
    [0, -1],   # State 0
    [0, 1],    # State 1
    [0, -1],   # State 2
    [0, 10],   # State 3 (goal state)
    [0, -1]    # State 4
])

# Q-learning update rule
def update_q_table(state, action, reward,
next_state):
    best_next_action =
np.argmax(Q_table[next_state])   # Best future
action
    Q_table[state, action] += learning_rate *
(reward + discount_factor * Q_table[next_state,
best_next_action] - Q_table[state, action])

# Simulating training loop
for episode in range(100):   # Train for 100
episodes
    state = np.random.randint(0, num_states)   #
Start at random state
    done = False
    while not done:
        action = np.random.choice([0, 1]) if
np.random.rand() < epsilon else
np.argmax(Q_table[state])
```

```
        next_state = state + action if state +
action < num_states else state  # Transition logic
        reward = reward_matrix[state, action]  #
Get reward
        update_q_table(state, action, reward,
next_state)
        state = next_state
        done = state == 3  # Stop when goal state
is reached

print("Trained Q-table:\n", Q_table)
```

This example illustrates how an agent **learns from interaction**, updates its Q-values, and eventually finds **optimal actions** to maximize long-term rewards.

Policy-Based Learning

Policy-based learning takes a different approach. Instead of estimating values and selecting actions based on them, policy-based methods **learn a direct mapping from states to actions**.

How Policy-Based Learning Works

The agent maintains a **policy function**, denoted as $\pi(a|s)$\pi(a \mid s), which defines the probability of selecting action **a** in state **s**. Instead of choosing actions based on stored values, the policy function determines actions directly.

There are two types of policies:

Deterministic Policy: Always selects the same action for a given state.

Stochastic Policy: Assigns probabilities to actions, allowing for exploration.

Policy-based methods are particularly useful in:

Continuous action spaces, where selecting actions from a predefined set is impractical.

High-dimensional environments, such as controlling robotic arms or playing complex strategy games.

Policy Gradient Methods

A popular class of policy-based methods is **policy gradient algorithms**, which update the policy based on the expected return from different actions. One widely used method is **REINFORCE**, which adjusts the policy using **gradient ascent** to maximize expected rewards.

The policy is updated using the equation:

$$\theta \leftarrow \theta + \alpha \nabla J(\theta)$$

where:

θ represents the policy parameters.

$J(\theta)$ is the expected reward.

α is the learning rate.

$\nabla J(\theta)$ is the gradient of the reward function with respect to policy parameters.

Example: Robot Arm Control

Consider a **robotic arm** that learns to pick up objects. Using a **policy-based approach**, it continuously adjusts its motion to achieve smooth, efficient grasping. Unlike value-based methods that rely on a finite set of actions, policy-based learning allows the arm to select movements from a continuous range of motions.

Choosing Between Value-Based and Policy-Based Learning

Value-based methods, such as Q-learning and Deep Q-Networks (DQN), are effective when:

The environment has **discrete** states and actions.

The agent needs to explore different states before committing to an optimal policy.

Training efficiency is a priority.

Policy-based methods, such as **REINFORCE** and **Proximal Policy Optimization (PPO)**, are better when:

The action space is **continuous** and cannot be easily discretized.

The environment is highly **complex and dynamic**, making value estimation difficult.

The agent needs **smooth, adaptive behavior** rather than predefined action selections.

Both approaches are foundational in reinforcement learning and are often **combined** in advanced models, such as **Actor-Critic methods**, which incorporate both value estimation and policy learning to improve stability and performance.

Q-Learning, Deep Q-Networks (DQN), and Actor-Critic Methods

Reinforcement Learning (RL) is a powerful machine learning technique that enables an **agent** to learn optimal actions by interacting with an environment. The agent receives **rewards** or **penalties** based on its actions and aims to maximize cumulative rewards over time.

One of the fundamental challenges in RL is learning **which actions lead to the highest long-term rewards**. Several algorithms have been developed to address this, with **Q-Learning, Deep Q-Networks (DQN), and Actor-Critic methods** being among the most widely used. Each of these methods has strengths suited to different types of problems.

Q-Learning: A Fundamental Value-Based Algorithm

Q-learning is a **model-free, value-based reinforcement learning algorithm** that helps an agent learn the optimal **action-selection policy** for maximizing cumulative rewards. It does this by maintaining a **Q-table**, which stores the expected rewards for taking an action in a given state.

The core idea behind Q-learning is to **iteratively update the Q-values** based on the rewards received and the expected future rewards from subsequent actions. The algorithm follows the **Bellman Equation**, which defines the relationship between current and future rewards:

$$Q(s, a) = Q(s, a) + \alpha \Big(R(s, a) + \gamma \max_{a'} Q(s', a') - Q(s, a) \Big)$$

where:

$Q(s,a)Q(s, a)$ is the current estimate of the value of taking action **aa** in state **ss**.

α\alpha (learning rate) determines how much new experiences override previous knowledge.

$R(s,a)R(s, a)$ is the **immediate reward** received after taking action **aa** in state **ss**.

γ\gamma (discount factor) balances **immediate vs. future rewards**.

$\max_{a'} a'Q(s',a')$\max_{a'} $Q(s', a')$ represents the **maximum expected future reward** from the next state s's'.

How Q-Learning Works

The agent **starts at a state** ss.

It **selects an action** aa using an **exploration-exploitation strategy** (e.g., ϵ\epsilon-greedy).

It **observes the reward** $R(s,a)R(s, a)$ and the **new state** s's'.

It **updates the Q-value** using the Bellman equation.

It repeats the process until it learns an optimal policy.

Example: Q-Learning for Grid Navigation

Consider a simple robot moving in a **5×5 grid** where:

The robot receives **+10 reward** for reaching the goal.

It receives **-1 penalty** for hitting an obstacle.

It starts at a random position and must learn the best path.

Let's implement **Q-learning** in Python for this environment.

```
import numpy as np
import random

# Define environment
grid_size = 5
num_states = grid_size * grid_size
```

```
num_actions = 4   # Up, Down, Left, Right

# Initialize Q-table
Q_table = np.zeros((num_states, num_actions))
learning_rate = 0.1
discount_factor = 0.9
epsilon = 0.1  # Exploration rate

# Define rewards and transitions
goal_state = 24  # Bottom-right corner
reward_matrix = np.full(num_states, -1)  # Default
penalty
reward_matrix[goal_state] = 10  # Goal reward

# Training loop
for episode in range(1000):
    state = random.randint(0, num_states - 1)  #
Start at random state
    done = False

    while not done:
        action = np.random.choice(num_actions) if
np.random.rand() < epsilon else
np.argmax(Q_table[state])
        next_state = max(0, min(num_states - 1,
state + (action - 1)))  # Transition logic
        reward = reward_matrix[next_state]
        Q_table[state, action] += learning_rate *
(reward + discount_factor *
np.max(Q_table[next_state]) - Q_table[state,
action])
        state = next_state
        done = (state == goal_state)

print("Trained Q-table:\n", Q_table)
```

This example shows how Q-learning enables an agent to **learn from experience** and build an optimal policy over time.

Deep Q-Networks (DQN): Scaling Q-Learning with Neural Networks

Why Q-Learning Fails in Complex Environments

Q-learning works well in simple problems but struggles when:

The state space is too large, making it impossible to store all Q-values in a table.

Continuous action spaces exist, where discrete Q-values cannot capture optimal behaviors.

Training is unstable, as Q-value updates depend on frequently changing estimates.

To address these challenges, **Deep Q-Networks (DQN)** replace the Q-table with a **neural network** that approximates Q-values.

Key Innovations in DQN

DQN introduces several improvements:

Experience Replay: Stores past experiences in a buffer and samples random mini-batches to reduce correlation between consecutive updates.

Target Networks: Uses a separate, slower-updating network to provide more stable Q-value targets.

Neural Network Approximation: Uses deep learning to estimate Q-values efficiently in high-dimensional spaces.

Implementing a Basic DQN

```
import tensorflow as tf
import numpy as np

class DQN:
    def __init__(self, state_size, action_size):
        self.model = tf.keras.Sequential([
            tf.keras.layers.Dense(24,
activation='relu', input_shape=(state_size,)),
            tf.keras.layers.Dense(24,
activation='relu'),
            tf.keras.layers.Dense(action_size,
activation='linear')
        ])
```

```
self.model.compile(optimizer=tf.keras.optimizers.Ad
am(learning_rate=0.01), loss='mse')

    def train(self, state, target):
        self.model.fit(state, target, epochs=1,
verbose=0)

# Example usage
dqn = DQN(state_size=4, action_size=2)
```

This demonstrates how a **deep neural network** can approximate Q-values, enabling learning in complex environments.

Actor-Critic Methods: Combining Value-Based and Policy-Based Learning

Both value-based (Q-learning, DQN) and policy-based (REINFORCE) methods have limitations:

Value-based methods are unstable in high-dimensional spaces.

Policy-based methods can have high variance and slow convergence.

Actor-Critic methods combine both approaches by maintaining:

An Actor (Policy Network): Determines which actions to take.

A Critic (Value Network): Evaluates how good those actions are.

This structure allows the agent to **learn policies more efficiently** while also benefiting from value estimates for stability.

Advantage Actor-Critic (A2C) Implementation

```
import tensorflow as tf

class ActorCritic:
    def __init__(self, state_size, action_size):
        self.actor = tf.keras.Sequential([
            tf.keras.layers.Dense(24,
activation='relu', input_shape=(state_size,)),
```

```
                tf.keras.layers.Dense(action_size,
activation='softmax')
        ])
        self.critic = tf.keras.Sequential([
            tf.keras.layers.Dense(24,
activation='relu', input_shape=(state_size,)),
            tf.keras.layers.Dense(1,
activation='linear')
        ])

    def train(self, state, action, reward,
next_state):
        value = self.critic.predict(state)
        target = reward + 0.9 *
self.critic.predict(next_state)
        advantage = target - value
        self.actor.fit(state, action,
sample_weight=advantage, verbose=0)
        self.critic.fit(state, target, verbose=0)
```

This method ensures both **stable learning** and **efficient exploration** in complex environments.

Q-learning, Deep Q-Networks, and Actor-Critic methods provide different approaches to learning optimal policies.

Q-learning is effective for small environments.

DQN extends Q-learning using neural networks for large state spaces.

Actor-Critic methods combine value and policy learning for more efficient learning in continuous, high-dimensional environments.

Choosing the right method depends on the complexity of the problem and the type of environment the agent must learn in.

3. Expanding to Multi-Agent Systems

Reinforcement Learning (RL) has proven effective for training individual agents to navigate complex environments, optimize decisions, and learn optimal strategies through rewards and penalties. However, real-world scenarios often involve **multiple agents** interacting in the same environment. These agents may need to **cooperate**, **compete**, or balance both strategies to achieve their objectives.

Multi-Agent Reinforcement Learning (MARL) extends standard RL by introducing **multiple learning agents** into a shared environment, where each agent's actions influence the learning and decision-making process of others. Unlike single-agent RL, where the environment is considered static apart from the agent's actions, MARL environments are **dynamic and continuously changing** as multiple agents adapt their behaviors simultaneously.

This chapter explores the core aspects of MARL, focusing on **cooperative vs. competitive learning**, **communication and coordination**, and **real-world case studies** demonstrating the power of multi-agent AI.

Cooperative and Competitive Learning in Multi-Agent Systems

When multiple AI agents operate within the same environment, their interactions significantly impact the learning process. Some agents work together to achieve a shared objective, while others compete for individual rewards. These two fundamental approaches are known as **cooperative learning** and **competitive learning**.

Both learning strategies are widely used in **multi-agent reinforcement learning (MARL)**, where multiple autonomous entities interact with an environment and optimize their behavior through rewards and penalties. Understanding these concepts is essential for designing AI systems that operate in **shared, interactive environments** like autonomous driving, robotics, financial trading, and multiplayer gaming.

This discussion explores the key principles of **cooperative and competitive learning**, their real-world applications, and the challenges associated with each approach.

Cooperative Learning

Cooperative learning occurs when multiple agents **work together toward a common goal**. The agents may have identical objectives or complementary tasks that require collaboration. Their learning process is structured so that successful cooperation leads to optimal performance for the entire group.

In cooperative settings, agents often **share rewards**, meaning that the success of one agent benefits all others. This approach is useful in scenarios where **teamwork and coordination** are necessary for achieving a shared objective.

How Cooperative Learning Works

In a cooperative learning environment:

Agents interact with the environment and take actions based on their policies.

They receive **group rewards** rather than individual rewards.

The success of an agent depends on how well it collaborates with others.

The learning process aims to **optimize collective performance** rather than individual gains.

Example: Multi-Robot Warehouse System

Consider a **warehouse with multiple autonomous robots** responsible for sorting, picking, and transporting packages. To maximize efficiency:

Robots must coordinate their paths to **avoid collisions**.

They need to **prioritize urgent deliveries** together.

They must communicate to **distribute tasks efficiently**.

Since the overall goal is to minimize delivery time and optimize warehouse operations, **agents receive a shared reward** based on the system's efficiency rather than individual performance.

Algorithms for Cooperative Learning

34

1. Centralized Training with Decentralized Execution (CTDE)

This is a common strategy where agents are trained with **access to global information** but operate independently once deployed. It allows for improved coordination while ensuring scalability.

2. Value Decomposition Networks (VDN) and QMIX

These are deep reinforcement learning techniques that **decompose a joint value function** into individual agent contributions, ensuring that agents learn to collaborate while optimizing global performance.

3. Multi-Agent Deep Deterministic Policy Gradient (MADDPG)

MADDPG extends traditional deep reinforcement learning to multi-agent settings by training agents with **shared or opponent-aware critics**, which help them understand the impact of others' actions.

Competitive Learning

Competitive learning occurs when agents **compete against one another**, each seeking to maximize its own reward, often at the expense of others. In this scenario, an agent's success typically means another agent's failure.

Competitive learning is commonly seen in **zero-sum games**, where one agent's gain results in an equal loss for another agent. These environments encourage **strategic decision-making, adversarial behavior, and adaptation** to opponents' actions.

How Competitive Learning Works

In a competitive learning environment:

Agents act **independently**, optimizing their own rewards rather than a shared objective.

The environment is adversarial, meaning that **one agent's gain often corresponds to another agent's loss**.

Agents **observe and react to opponents**, adapting their strategies accordingly.

The goal is to **outperform competitors** through better decision-making and adaptation.

Example: AI in Strategic Gaming (StarCraft II, Chess, Dota 2)

Competitive learning is widely used in **strategy-based AI**, where intelligent agents must develop **winning strategies against opponents**.

For example, in **StarCraft II**, an AI-controlled agent must:

Manage resources efficiently while preventing opponents from gaining an advantage.

Predict and counter enemy strategies in real time.

Adapt to changing game conditions based on opponents' moves.

The AI **continuously improves its strategy** by learning from past games and competing against stronger opponents through **self-play**, where it repeatedly plays against copies of itself.

Algorithms for Competitive Learning

1. Self-Play Reinforcement Learning

In self-play, an agent repeatedly trains against its own past versions, ensuring that it constantly improves. This approach was used in **DeepMind's AlphaGo**, which defeated human world champions in the board game Go.

2. Minimax-Q Learning

This is an extension of Q-learning designed for competitive environments. It optimizes decisions **assuming that opponents will always choose the best counter-strategy**.

3. Proximal Policy Optimization (PPO) for Competitive Environments

PPO helps agents **learn robust strategies** by balancing exploration and exploitation in competitive settings, making it effective in adversarial tasks.

Cooperative vs. Competitive Learning: Key Differences

Feature	Cooperative Learning	Competitive Learning
Objective	Achieve a common goal	Outperform opponents
Reward Structure	Shared reward across agents	Individual reward per agent
Agent Interaction	Coordination and collaboration	Adversarial behavior
Strategy Focus	Optimizing collective performance	Winning against opponents
Common Applications	Robotics, multi-agent traffic systems, smart grids	Game AI, trading bots, military simulations

Mixed Learning Environments: Combining Cooperation and Competition

Many real-world environments are **not purely cooperative or competitive**, but instead contain **elements of both**.

For example, in **autonomous driving**, self-driving cars must:

Cooperate by following traffic rules and preventing accidents.

Compete for limited road space at intersections.

Similarly, in **financial markets**, trading algorithms may:

Cooperate by ensuring market stability.

Compete to achieve higher profits for their investors.

To handle mixed environments, **hybrid MARL algorithms** use a combination of cooperative and competitive strategies, allowing agents to adjust their behavior based on the situation.

Challenges in Cooperative and Competitive Learning

Credit Assignment Problem – When multiple agents contribute to success, it is difficult to determine which agent's actions were most beneficial.

Scalability – As the number of agents increases, coordination becomes more complex.

Communication Overhead – If agents rely on explicit communication, the system must ensure efficient message passing.

Challenges in Competitive Learning

Exploitability – If an agent follows predictable patterns, opponents can exploit its weaknesses.

Non-Stationarity – As opponents learn and adapt, the environment constantly changes, making long-term planning difficult.

High Computational Costs – Training AI agents to compete in complex settings (e.g., real-time strategy games) requires extensive computing power.

Cooperative and competitive learning are two fundamental approaches in **multi-agent reinforcement learning (MARL)**. In **cooperative learning**, agents collaborate to achieve a shared goal, making it ideal for applications like **robotics, smart grids, and team-based problem-solving**. In **competitive learning**, agents compete to maximize their individual rewards, commonly used in **strategic gaming, trading, and adversarial AI**.

Many real-world systems require a **combination of cooperation and competition**, making hybrid learning strategies increasingly important. Advances in reinforcement learning continue to refine these approaches, allowing for **more sophisticated, intelligent multi-agent systems** capable of handling complex decision-making environments.

Communication and Coordination in Multi-Agent Environments

When multiple agents operate in the same environment, their ability to **communicate and coordinate** determines how effectively they achieve their objectives. Some agents may share a **common goal**, requiring them to work together, while others may have **competing interests**, where strategic interaction is necessary. Regardless of the scenario, the presence of multiple agents introduces complexity that **cannot be solved through individual learning alone**.

Why Communication and Coordination Matter in Multi-Agent Systems

Single-agent reinforcement learning (RL) operates under the assumption that an agent learns by interacting with a static environment. But in a **multi-agent system (MAS)**, the environment itself is dynamic because it consists of **other learning agents** who are also adapting their behaviors.

The challenges in these environments arise from the fact that each agent's **decisions affect the state of others**. For example, in a **self-driving car network**, one vehicle's decision to change lanes affects nearby vehicles, requiring them to react accordingly. In a **multi-robot warehouse**, efficient task execution depends on how well the robots coordinate without interfering with each other.

Two fundamental aspects make multi-agent interactions complex:

Communication – Agents exchanging information to make better decisions.

Coordination – Agents aligning their actions to avoid conflicts or inefficiencies.

Both aspects must be carefully designed because inefficient communication can introduce **redundant information** or slow down decision-making, while poor coordination can lead to **conflicting behaviors** that reduce overall efficiency.

Types of Communication in Multi-Agent Systems

Communication in multi-agent systems can be broadly categorized into **explicit** and **implicit** communication. The choice between the two depends on the application and the constraints of the environment.

Explicit Communication

Explicit communication occurs when agents directly share **messages or signals** with one another. This can be in the form of **predefined signals, structured messages, or learned representations**.

For example, in a multi-drone delivery system, each drone might **broadcast its position and intended path** to others to prevent collisions.

Implementation of Explicit Communication in a Multi-Agent Grid Environment

Let's implement a simple **multi-agent grid** where agents communicate their intended actions to each other before execution. The goal is for two agents to move toward a target while avoiding collisions.

```python
import numpy as np

class MultiAgentGrid:
    def __init__(self, grid_size=5, target=(4, 4)):
        self.grid_size = grid_size
        self.target = target
        self.agent_positions = [(0, 0), (0, 1)]  #
Starting positions

    def step(self, actions):
        new_positions = []
        for i, (x, y) in
enumerate(self.agent_positions):
            if actions[i] == "up":
                x = max(0, x - 1)
            elif actions[i] == "down":
                x = min(self.grid_size - 1, x + 1)
            elif actions[i] == "left":
                y = max(0, y - 1)
            elif actions[i] == "right":
                y = min(self.grid_size - 1, y + 1)

            new_positions.append((x, y))

        # Prevent collisions by checking if both
agents move to the same spot
        if new_positions[0] == new_positions[1]:
```

```
            return self.agent_positions  # Ignore
movement to avoid collision

        self.agent_positions = new_positions
        return self.agent_positions

    def communicate(self):
        # Agents exchange their intended moves
before executing them
        intended_moves = ["right", "down"]  #
Example communication
        return intended_moves

# Example execution
env = MultiAgentGrid()
actions = env.communicate()
new_positions = env.step(actions)
print("New agent positions:", new_positions)
```

In this example, both agents communicate **their intended actions** before executing them, helping prevent **conflicts** and **optimizing movement**. This type of explicit messaging is used in real-world applications like **autonomous drones coordinating in airspace** or **traffic lights sharing data to optimize signal timing**.

Implicit Communication

Not all communication needs to be explicit. In many cases, agents infer what others intend to do **by observing their behavior** rather than exchanging direct messages. This is called **implicit communication**.

A common example is **human teamwork**: In a soccer match, players do not always shout instructions at each other. Instead, they **observe movements, predict behaviors, and adjust accordingly**.

Implicit communication is particularly useful when:

Communication bandwidth is limited. (e.g., space exploration where direct messaging is costly)

Agents need to be more adaptable. (e.g., AI teammates in video games learning player habits)

A reinforcement learning approach called **emergent communication** allows agents to develop their own signals by associating observed behaviors with outcomes.

Coordination in Multi-Agent Systems

Communication alone does not guarantee success. Agents also need to **coordinate their actions** to ensure they achieve optimal outcomes.

There are multiple approaches to achieving coordination:

Centralized vs. Decentralized Coordination

A **centralized approach** relies on a **global controller** that collects information from all agents, computes optimal actions, and then directs the agents. While this method ensures optimal coordination, it is computationally expensive and does not scale well with many agents.

A **decentralized approach**, on the other hand, allows each agent to **make independent decisions** while aligning with the overall goal. This is more scalable but introduces challenges in ensuring that agents act in harmony.

Case Study: Multi-Agent Traffic Signal Optimization

Traffic signal control is a complex problem where each signal must **adjust its timing dynamically** to minimize congestion. A decentralized MARL approach allows each traffic light to act independently while considering nearby signals.

A reinforcement learning-based traffic light system might:

Observe **traffic flow** using cameras and sensors.

Adjust signal timing **based on real-time congestion data**.

Communicate with adjacent traffic lights to **optimize network-wide efficiency**.

Through MARL training, each signal learns to balance **cooperation (smoother overall traffic flow)** and **competition (optimizing its own intersection)**.

Challenges in Multi-Agent Communication and Coordination

Designing effective communication and coordination in multi-agent systems presents several challenges:

Scalability Issues

As the number of agents increases, communication overhead grows. If each agent sends messages to all others, the system may become **overloaded with redundant information**.

Solutions such as **hierarchical communication** (where only key agents relay information) or **attention mechanisms** (where agents selectively listen to important peers) can reduce complexity.

Learning to Trust Communication

Agents may share unreliable or self-serving information in competitive settings. This problem is seen in **financial markets**, where trading bots may manipulate prices through misleading signals.

Approaches such as **credibility scoring** (assigning trust values to agents based on past actions) can improve reliability.

Handling Partial Observability

In many real-world environments, agents do not have access to **complete state information**. Autonomous vehicles, for example, must make driving decisions based on **limited sensor data**.

Using **POMDPs (Partially Observable Markov Decision Processes)**, agents can **infer missing information** through past experiences, improving decision-making despite uncertainty.

Communication and coordination are essential in **multi-agent reinforcement learning** because they determine how well agents function together in complex environments. Whether through **explicit messaging** or **implicit**

observation, agents must exchange information effectively while balancing cooperation and competition.

Real-world applications of these concepts include **autonomous traffic control, swarm robotics, AI-driven trading, and multi-agent gaming**. As reinforcement learning research progresses, new techniques for efficient **agent interaction, decentralized decision-making, and adaptive coordination** will continue to improve the performance of intelligent multi-agent systems.

Case Studies in Multi-Agent AI

Multi-Agent Artificial Intelligence (AI) has been applied in various industries where multiple autonomous systems interact with each other. These applications range from **robotics and autonomous vehicles** to **gaming, finance, and smart infrastructure**. Each of these domains presents unique challenges, requiring advanced coordination, decision-making, and learning strategies.

This discussion will explore real-world case studies where multi-agent AI is used, highlighting how agents communicate, learn, and adapt within complex environments.

1. Multi-Agent Systems in Robotics: Amazon Warehouse Robots

In large-scale warehouses, such as those operated by **Amazon**, thousands of robots work together to transport goods efficiently. These robots are designed to pick up, move, and sort packages while avoiding collisions and optimizing delivery times. Managing such a **multi-agent robotic system** requires **real-time coordination, path planning, and efficient resource allocation**.

Challenges and Solutions

One of the biggest challenges in warehouse automation is **efficient navigation**. Since multiple robots share the same environment, they must coordinate their movements to avoid congestion.

To address this, Amazon's robotic system uses:

Multi-Agent Pathfinding Algorithms to ensure that robots do not collide while navigating to their destinations.

Decentralized Control Mechanisms that allow each robot to make local decisions while following global optimization rules.

Reinforcement Learning (RL) to improve task allocation, ensuring that the nearest available robot handles incoming orders.

Technical Implementation

The warehouse is modeled as a **grid environment**, where each robot acts as an agent that follows RL-based policies. The reward function encourages robots to:

Minimize travel time to targets.

Avoid collisions with other robots.

Optimize package retrieval efficiency.

A simplified **Python simulation** for multi-agent warehouse navigation can be implemented using Q-learning:

```python
import numpy as np
import random

# Grid size
grid_size = 5
num_robots = 3
goal_positions = [(4, 4), (3, 3), (2, 2)]  #
Targets for each robot

# Q-table for each robot
Q_tables = [np.zeros((grid_size, grid_size, 4)) for
_ in range(num_robots)]

# Actions: Up, Down, Left, Right
actions = [(-1, 0), (1, 0), (0, -1), (0, 1)]

def step(position, action):
    """Move robot while keeping it within grid
boundaries."""
```

```
    x, y = position
    dx, dy = actions[action]
    x, y = max(0, min(grid_size - 1, x + dx)),
max(0, min(grid_size - 1, y + dy))
    return (x, y)

# Simulating robots moving towards their goals
for episode in range(1000):
    robot_positions = [(random.randint(0,
grid_size-1), random.randint(0, grid_size-1)) for _
in range(num_robots)]
    done = False

    while not done:
        for i in range(num_robots):
            action = random.choice(range(4))    #
Random move
            new_position = step(robot_positions[i],
action)

            # Reward system
            if new_position == goal_positions[i]:
                reward = 10   # Goal reached
                done = True
            else:
                reward = -1   # Penalize movement

            Q_tables[i][robot_positions[i][0],
robot_positions[i][1], action] += 0.1 * (reward +
0.9 * np.max(Q_tables[i][new_position[0],
new_position[1]]) -
Q_tables[i][robot_positions[i][0],
robot_positions[i][1], action])
            robot_positions[i] = new_position
```

This simulation demonstrates how reinforcement learning can be applied to warehouse robots that **optimize movement, avoid congestion, and improve efficiency** through a cooperative multi-agent system.

2. Multi-Agent AI in Autonomous Vehicles: Self-Driving Car Coordination

Self-driving cars must operate in a **shared environment**, where their actions affect other vehicles, pedestrians, and traffic systems. To ensure safety and efficiency, **multi-agent reinforcement learning (MARL)** is used to teach cars how to:

Merge into traffic smoothly.

React to other vehicles' behaviors.

Negotiate intersections efficiently.

Challenges and Solutions

Non-Stationarity: Since each car is continuously learning and updating its strategy, the environment is always changing. Advanced RL techniques, such as **centralized training with decentralized execution (CTDE)**, help stabilize learning.

Safety Constraints: Cars must learn to balance **speed and safety**, avoiding risky maneuvers. Reward functions in MARL models penalize unsafe actions.

Communication: Vehicles share limited information, such as **speed, position, and intended maneuvers**, to improve coordination.

Case Study: DeepMind's Traffic Optimization Model

DeepMind developed a MARL-based model where self-driving cars were trained using **Multi-Agent Deep Deterministic Policy Gradients (MADDPG)**. The system helped cars learn:

How to optimize lane merging.

How to anticipate other drivers' behaviors.

How to react to sudden obstacles without causing accidents.

Real-World Application

Tesla and Waymo integrate **multi-agent decision-making algorithms** into their self-driving systems. These algorithms allow cars to coordinate actions without requiring centralized control.

3. Multi-Agent AI in Finance: Algorithmic Trading Systems

In financial markets, **automated trading agents** make buy and sell decisions based on market trends. These agents compete and cooperate, reacting to fluctuations in stock prices.

Challenges and Solutions

Market Fluctuations: Agents must predict price changes based on historical data.

High-Speed Decision Making: Trading decisions are made in milliseconds, requiring efficient RL models.

Competitive Learning: Agents continuously adapt to **other traders' behaviors**, making the market environment dynamic.

Technical Approach

Reinforcement learning algorithms, such as PPO (Proximal Policy Optimization), are used to train trading agents to maximize profits while managing risks.

A **multi-agent stock trading environment** can be simulated using RL models where:

Agents are trained to **compete for market advantage**.

They learn **optimal trading strategies** through **historical data analysis**.

Large hedge funds like Citadel and Renaissance Technologies use AI-driven multi-agent systems to **execute trades, detect patterns, and minimize risk** in financial markets.

4. Multi-Agent AI in Gaming: OpenAI Five in Dota 2

One of the most successful applications of MARL in gaming is **OpenAI Five**, an AI system trained to play **Dota 2** at a superhuman level. Unlike traditional games like Chess or Go, Dota 2 is a **real-time strategy game** requiring:

Coordination between **multiple AI-controlled characters**.

Decision-making under uncertainty.

Balancing **cooperation and competition**.

Training Approach

OpenAI trained **five AI agents** using reinforcement learning techniques such as **self-play** and **policy gradient optimization**.

Each agent learned how to **cooperate with teammates** while competing against opponents.

The AI played **180 years' worth of games per day**, continuously refining its strategies.

Key Outcomes

OpenAI Five defeated professional human players in **5v5 matches**.

The AI developed strategies that were **unconventional yet highly effective**.

It demonstrated that **MARL can handle high-dimensional, real-time decision-making environments**.

This case study highlights how **multi-agent AI can master complex human-designed environments**, leading to breakthroughs in AI coordination and competition.

Multi-agent AI is transforming various industries by **enabling autonomous systems to collaborate, compete, and adapt** in shared environments.

In robotics, MARL improves warehouse automation.

In self-driving cars, MARL enables vehicles to coordinate safely.

In finance, MARL powers AI-driven trading.

In gaming, MARL leads to superhuman AI performance.

As research progresses, **more advanced coordination techniques, communication models, and learning strategies** will further improve how multiple AI agents operate together in dynamic and complex environments.

4. Value-Based MARL Methods

Multi-Agent Reinforcement Learning (MARL) introduces additional complexity compared to single-agent RL because agents must learn while interacting with other learning entities. One of the most effective approaches for MARL is **value-based learning**, where agents estimate the expected rewards of different actions and choose the ones that maximize their long-term success.

In traditional RL, value-based methods like Q-learning allow a single agent to update its Q-values based on the rewards received from an environment. However, when multiple agents are involved, each agent's decisions impact not only its own future but also the experiences of others. This creates challenges such as non-stationarity, credit assignment, and scalability.

This chapter explores value-based MARL methods, comparing Independent Q-learning with Centralized Q-learning, introducing Multi-Agent Deep Q-Networks (MADQN), and examining the challenges of value decomposition, which arise when trying to distribute rewards across multiple agents fairly and efficiently.

Independent Q-Learning and Centralized Q-Learning

Multi-Agent Reinforcement Learning (MARL) introduces a level of complexity far beyond what single-agent reinforcement learning deals with. When multiple agents interact in the same environment, their actions affect not only their own outcomes but also the learning process of other agents. This creates a highly dynamic system where each agent must continuously adapt to changes caused by others.

One of the fundamental challenges in MARL is **how agents should learn**. Should each agent learn its own strategy independently, treating others as part of the environment? Or should all agents learn together in a centralized manner, accounting for each other's actions? These two approaches are known as **Independent Q-Learning (IQL)** and **Centralized Q-Learning**.

Both approaches have advantages and limitations, depending on the problem at hand.

Independent Q-Learning (IQL)

Independent Q-learning (IQL) is an extension of standard **Q-learning**, a reinforcement learning technique where an agent learns by updating a **Q-table** that stores expected rewards for different actions in various states. In IQL, each agent **learns independently**, treating all other agents as part of the environment rather than explicitly considering their learning processes.

How IQL Works

In IQL, each agent maintains its own **Q-function**, which is updated using the **Bellman equation**:

$$Q_i(s, a) = Q_i(s, a) + \alpha \left(R + \gamma \max_{a'} Q_i(s', a') - Q_i(s, a) \right)$$

where:

$Q_i(s, a)$ represents the Q-value for agent i in state s when taking action a.

R is the immediate reward received after taking action a.

γ is the discount factor, controlling how much future rewards influence current decisions.

$\max_{a'} Q_i(s', a')$ estimates the best possible future reward.

α is the learning rate, controlling how much the agent updates its values.

Each agent updates its own Q-table without explicitly considering that other agents are also learning. This means that from each agent's perspective, the environment appears **non-stationary** because the policies of other agents change over time.

Real-World Application: Multi-Robot Exploration

A good example of independent Q-learning is in **multi-robot exploration**, where multiple autonomous robots explore an unknown environment to build a map or locate targets. Each robot moves independently, using its own Q-learning algorithm to navigate without requiring explicit coordination with others.

For instance, in disaster response, a fleet of robots might be deployed to map a collapsed building. Each robot explores its surroundings independently while avoiding obstacles. Since the robots do not explicitly communicate, their policies evolve separately, leading to **emergent coordination**—where agents indirectly cooperate by adjusting their behaviors based on observations.

Code Example: Multi-Agent IQL in a Grid Environment

Let's implement a **simple multi-agent IQL system**, where two agents navigate a grid independently to reach a goal.

```python
import numpy as np
import random

# Environment settings
grid_size = 5
num_agents = 2
num_actions = 4   # Up, Down, Left, Right
goal_position = (4, 4)

# Q-tables for each agent
Q_tables = [np.zeros((grid_size, grid_size,
num_actions)) for _ in range(num_agents)]
learning_rate = 0.1
discount_factor = 0.9
epsilon = 0.1   # Exploration rate

# Actions mapping
actions = [(-1, 0), (1, 0), (0, -1), (0, 1)]

def step(position, action):
    """Move agent while staying within
boundaries."""
    x, y = position
    dx, dy = actions[action]
    x = max(0, min(grid_size - 1, x + dx))
    y = max(0, min(grid_size - 1, y + dy))
    return (x, y)
```

```
# Training loop
for episode in range(1000):
    agent_positions = [(random.randint(0, grid_size
- 1), random.randint(0, grid_size - 1)) for _ in
range(num_agents)]
    done = False

    while not done:
        for i in range(num_agents):
            state = agent_positions[i]
            action =
np.random.choice(range(num_actions)) if
np.random.rand() < epsilon else
np.argmax(Q_tables[i][state[0], state[1]])
            new_position = step(state, action)

            # Reward system
            if new_position == goal_position:
                reward = 10  # Goal reached
                done = True
            else:
                reward = -1  # Penalize movement

            # Update Q-table
            Q_tables[i][state[0], state[1], action]
+= learning_rate * (reward + discount_factor *
np.max(Q_tables[i][new_position[0],
new_position[1]]) - Q_tables[i][state[0], state[1],
action])
            agent_positions[i] = new_position

print("Trained Q-tables for agents:\n", Q_tables)
```

This simulation shows how independent agents navigate separately, adjusting their behaviors without explicit coordination. While this works in simple settings, in more complex environments, **agents may struggle with coordination and efficiency**.

Centralized Q-Learning

Centralized Q-learning addresses the limitations of IQL by **training agents together**, considering all agents' actions when updating Q-values. Instead of treating others as part of the environment, centralized learning explicitly models the interactions between agents.

In centralized Q-learning, the update rule modifies the Q-value function to include **all agents' actions**:

$$Q(s, a_1, a_2, ..., a_n) = Q(s, a_1, a_2, ..., a_n) + \alpha \left(R + \gamma \max_{a'_1, a'_2, ..., a'_n} Q(s', a'_1, a'_2, ..., a'_n) - Q(s, a_1, a_2, ..., a_n) \right)$$

where:

$Q(s, a_1, a_2, ..., a_n)$ represents the **joint Q-value**, considering all agents' actions.

Agents receive a **shared reward**, promoting cooperative behavior.

Real-World Application: Autonomous Traffic Coordination

A practical use of centralized Q-learning is in **autonomous traffic signal optimization**, where multiple traffic lights must adjust their timing dynamically to minimize congestion. Since all signals are interdependent, a **centralized learning system** models their interactions to find an optimal strategy.

By considering all traffic lights as a single system, centralized Q-learning ensures that:

The overall traffic flow is improved rather than each intersection optimizing independently.

Decisions made by one signal do not negatively impact the next signal.

Challenges of Centralized Q-Learning

Computational Complexity – The number of state-action pairs increases exponentially with the number of agents, making it **difficult to scale**.

Data Sharing Requirements – All agents must share their experiences with a **centralized controller**, requiring **high bandwidth** and efficient communication.

Single Point of Failure – If the centralized system fails, all agents lose guidance, making the system less **resilient** compared to decentralized approaches.

Which Approach Works Best?

The choice between **independent Q-learning and centralized Q-learning** depends on the specific **requirements of the application**.

IQL is better for competitive environments or when agents operate in isolation (e.g., robotic exploration).

Centralized Q-learning is better for cooperative environments where agents must coordinate closely (e.g., traffic control, multi-robot assembly).

A hybrid approach, **Centralized Training with Decentralized Execution (CTDE)**, combines the best of both worlds. Agents train in a centralized manner but operate independently once deployed.

Multi-agent learning requires balancing **individual autonomy** with **global coordination**. While **independent Q-learning** is scalable and straightforward, it struggles in cooperative tasks. **Centralized Q-learning** improves collaboration but faces challenges with computational complexity. The best approach depends on the **nature of agent interactions and the level of coordination required**.

Multi-Agent Deep Q-Networks (MADQN)

Deep Q-Networks (DQN) revolutionized reinforcement learning by enabling agents to learn optimal strategies in high-dimensional environments using deep neural networks. However, when multiple agents interact within the same environment, traditional Q-learning methods become inefficient. Agents no longer operate in isolation, and their decisions influence the learning processes of others, creating a **non-stationary** environment where traditional single-agent DQN struggles to converge.

Multi-Agent Deep Q-Networks (MADQN) extend DQN to **multi-agent settings**, where agents learn not only from their individual experiences but also while adapting to the behaviors of other learning agents. This approach is widely used in **robotic coordination, autonomous driving, smart grid management, and cooperative AI-driven decision-making**.

Why Standard DQN Fails in Multi-Agent Environments

In a single-agent setting, DQN learns an optimal policy by mapping states to Q-values using a deep neural network. The Q-value function is updated iteratively using the Bellman equation:

$$Q(s, a) = Q(s, a) + \alpha \left(R + \gamma \max_{a'} Q(s', a') - Q(s, a) \right)$$

where:

$Q(s, a)$ is the estimated future reward for taking action a in state s.

R is the reward received after taking the action.

γ is the discount factor that balances short-term and long-term rewards.

α is the learning rate.

In a **multi-agent environment**, however, this approach fails because:

Non-Stationarity: Since multiple agents are learning simultaneously, the environment keeps changing, making it difficult for an individual agent to learn a stable policy.

Exploration Complexity: Agents need to explore not only their own action space but also account for how other agents' actions impact the environment.

Scalability Issues: The state-action space grows exponentially with the number of agents, making tabular Q-learning infeasible.

To address these issues, MADQN incorporates **neural network approximations, experience replay, and independent learning strategies** while ensuring agents adapt to one another's learning processes.

How Multi-Agent Deep Q-Networks (MADQN) Work

Neural Network-Based Q-Function Approximation

MADQN replaces the traditional Q-table with a **deep neural network (DNN)** that estimates Q-values. Each agent maintains its own DQN, which maps states to Q-values for different actions.

The **architecture** of a MADQN model typically consists of:

An **input layer** that processes the agent's observations (state).

Hidden layers that extract meaningful features from the state.

An **output layer** that produces Q-values for each possible action.

A neural network is trained to minimize the difference between its predicted Q-values and the target Q-values computed using:

$$\hat{Q}(s, a) = R + \gamma \max_{a'} Q(s', a')$$

where $\hat{Q}(s, a)$ is the target Q-value used to update the network.

Experience Replay to Improve Stability

In single-agent DQN, **experience replay** stores past experiences and samples them randomly to **break the correlation between consecutive experiences**. This prevents the network from overfitting to recent experiences and stabilizes training.

MADQN **extends experience replay** by allowing agents to share experiences or sample experiences in a way that balances learning across agents. This helps in environments where:

Some agents learn faster than others.

The environment changes unpredictably due to multiple agents' actions.

Target Networks for Stabilization

To prevent instability in Q-learning updates, MADQN uses a **target network**, which is a delayed copy of the main Q-network. This network is updated at fixed intervals, providing a more stable Q-value target.

Implementing MADQN in Python

To demonstrate MADQN, let's implement a **multi-agent environment** where two agents learn to navigate a shared grid while avoiding obstacles.

Step 1: Install Dependencies

Ensure that you have TensorFlow or PyTorch installed. We will use TensorFlow for this implementation:

```
pip install tensorflow numpy gym
```

Step 2: Define the Multi-Agent Environment

```python
import numpy as np
import random
import tensorflow as tf
from tensorflow import keras

# Define the multi-agent grid environment
class MultiAgentGrid:
    def __init__(self, grid_size=5, num_agents=2):
        self.grid_size = grid_size
        self.num_agents = num_agents
        self.agent_positions = [(0, 0), (grid_size
- 1, grid_size - 1)]  # Initial positions
        self.goal_positions = [(grid_size - 1,
grid_size - 1), (0, 0)]  # Goal positions

    def reset(self):
        self.agent_positions = [(0, 0),
(self.grid_size - 1, self.grid_size - 1)]
        return self.agent_positions

    def step(self, actions):
        new_positions = []
        for i, (x, y) in
enumerate(self.agent_positions):
            if actions[i] == "up":
                x = max(0, x - 1)
            elif actions[i] == "down":
                x = min(self.grid_size - 1, x + 1)
            elif actions[i] == "left":
                y = max(0, y - 1)
            elif actions[i] == "right":
```

```
                y = min(self.grid_size - 1, y + 1)
            new_positions.append((x, y))

        self.agent_positions = new_positions
        rewards = [10 if self.agent_positions[i] ==
self.goal_positions[i] else -1 for i in
range(self.num_agents)]
        return self.agent_positions, rewards

# Initialize the environment
env = MultiAgentGrid()
```

Step 3: Define the MADQN Model

```
class MADQN:
    def __init__(self, state_size, action_size):
        self.model = keras.Sequential([
            keras.layers.Dense(64,
activation='relu', input_shape=(state_size,)),
            keras.layers.Dense(64,
activation='relu'),
            keras.layers.Dense(action_size,
activation='linear')
        ])

self.model.compile(optimizer=keras.optimizers.Adam(
learning_rate=0.01), loss='mse')

    def train(self, state, target):
        self.model.fit(state, target, epochs=1,
verbose=0)

# Create separate networks for each agent
agent1 = MADQN(state_size=2, action_size=4)
agent2 = MADQN(state_size=2, action_size=4)
```

Step 4: Training Loop

```
num_episodes = 1000

epsilon = 0.1  # Exploration rate
```

```
for episode in range(num_episodes):
    state = env.reset()
    done = False

    while not done:
        actions = [
            np.random.choice(4) if np.random.rand()
< epsilon else
np.argmax(agent1.model.predict(np.array([state[0]])
)),
            np.random.choice(4) if np.random.rand()
< epsilon else
np.argmax(agent2.model.predict(np.array([state[1]])
))
        ]

        next_state, rewards = env.step(actions)

        # Train the agents
        target1 = rewards[0] + 0.9 *
np.max(agent1.model.predict(np.array([next_state[0]
])))
        target2 = rewards[1] + 0.9 *
np.max(agent2.model.predict(np.array([next_state[1]
])))

        agent1.train(np.array([state[0]]),
np.array([target1]))
        agent2.train(np.array([state[1]]),
np.array([target2]))

        state = next_state
        done = all(pos == goal for pos, goal in
zip(state, env.goal_positions))
```

MADQN extends Deep Q-Networks to **multi-agent reinforcement learning** by allowing agents to learn while considering interactions with others. It introduces **experience replay, target networks, and decentralized learning** to handle non-stationarity and improve learning efficiency.

This approach is widely used in **robotics, autonomous traffic systems, and AI-driven strategic decision-making**, making it an essential tool for developing **multi-agent intelligent systems**.

Challenges of Value Decomposition

In **multi-agent reinforcement learning (MARL)**, agents often need to work together to achieve a shared objective. Unlike single-agent reinforcement learning, where an agent optimizes its own policy based on individual rewards, cooperative MARL introduces **the challenge of distributing rewards** among multiple agents fairly and efficiently. This is where **value decomposition** comes into play.

Value decomposition methods attempt to break down a **global team reward** into **individual agent rewards** while preserving the overall optimal strategy. However, doing this correctly is difficult because of several fundamental challenges, including **credit assignment, scalability, non-stationarity, and function approximation errors**.

The Role of Value Decomposition in Multi-Agent Learning

When multiple agents collaborate in a reinforcement learning task, they often receive **a shared reward** rather than separate, individualized rewards. For example, in **autonomous drone swarms** coordinating to map an area, the success of the mission is evaluated collectively rather than based on each drone's contribution alone.

Without value decomposition, each agent would learn based only on the shared team reward. This makes it difficult to determine which agent's actions were beneficial, leading to inefficient learning. Value decomposition attempts to **assign each agent a fair portion of the total reward**, making training more effective.

However, the process is not straightforward. Agents interact with each other and the environment, creating **dependencies that make it difficult to isolate contributions**. This introduces several challenges that need to be addressed.

Challenge 1: The Credit Assignment Problem

The biggest issue with value decomposition is the **credit assignment problem**—determining how much each agent contributed to the overall success or failure of a task.

When multiple agents interact, their actions **overlap and influence each other's outcomes**. For example, in a **multi-agent robotic warehouse system**, if a package is delivered successfully, was it because one robot moved it efficiently, or because another robot made space for it? Assigning rewards fairly is difficult because contributions are **interdependent and not always directly observable**.

One way researchers address this challenge is through **counterfactual credit assignment**, where an agent's impact is measured by comparing what happened **with and without its actions**. This requires modeling alternative scenarios, which adds complexity to the learning process.

Let's look at a simple Python implementation of **counterfactual credit assignment** in a grid environment where two agents cooperate to reach a target:

```python
import numpy as np

# Define environment
class MultiAgentGrid:
    def __init__(self, grid_size=5):
        self.grid_size = grid_size
        self.agent_positions = [(0, 0), (0, 1)]
        self.goal_position = (4, 4)

    def reset(self):
        self.agent_positions = [(0, 0), (0, 1)]
        return self.agent_positions

    def step(self, actions):
        new_positions = []
        for i, (x, y) in enumerate(self.agent_positions):
            if actions[i] == "up":
                x = max(0, x - 1)
            elif actions[i] == "down":
                x = min(self.grid_size - 1, x + 1)
```

```python
            elif actions[i] == "left":
                y = max(0, y - 1)
            elif actions[i] == "right":
                y = min(self.grid_size - 1, y + 1)
            new_positions.append((x, y))

        self.agent_positions = new_positions
        reward = 10 if self.agent_positions[0] ==
self.goal_position or self.agent_positions[1] ==
self.goal_position else -1
        return self.agent_positions, reward

# Counterfactual credit assignment
def counterfactual_reward(env, original_actions):
    original_reward = env.step(original_actions)[1]

    counterfactual_rewards = []
    for i in range(len(original_actions)):
        temp_actions = original_actions.copy()
        temp_actions[i] = np.random.choice(["up",
"down", "left", "right"])   # Random alternative
action
        altered_reward = env.step(temp_actions)[1]

counterfactual_rewards.append(original_reward -
altered_reward)   # Measure impact of agent's action

    return counterfactual_rewards

# Example usage
env = MultiAgentGrid()
state = env.reset()
actions = ["right", "down"]
cf_rewards = counterfactual_reward(env, actions)
print("Counterfactual rewards:", cf_rewards)
```

This simple implementation estimates how much each agent's action **contributed to the final reward** by comparing different possible outcomes. However, in real-world applications, computing counterfactuals for every possible action is computationally expensive.

Challenge 2: Non-Stationarity in Multi-Agent Learning

In single-agent reinforcement learning, the environment remains **fixed** except for changes caused by the agent's actions. In multi-agent systems, however, the environment is **constantly changing** because every agent is also learning and updating its strategy at the same time. This makes value decomposition more difficult because reward assignments can become **unstable**.

For example, in a **multi-agent self-driving car simulation**, if one car learns to slow down at intersections while another learns to speed up, the learning process becomes unpredictable. The reward function may keep shifting, preventing stable learning.

To address this, some algorithms like **QMIX (Q-Mixing Networks)** enforce a constraint where the total Q-value function is a **monotonic combination** of individual Q-values, ensuring that changes in one agent's policy do not drastically alter reward assignments.

Challenge 3: Scalability with Increasing Agents

As the number of agents increases, **the complexity of value decomposition grows exponentially**. If there are 10 agents in an environment, the joint Q-function must consider all 10 agents' actions, leading to an **explosion in state-action pairs**.

One way to handle this is through **decentralized execution**, where training is centralized, but execution is decentralized. This is known as **Centralized Training with Decentralized Execution (CTDE)**. It allows agents to learn **joint strategies** during training while operating **independently** during execution.

A practical example of scalability issues is seen in **multi-agent energy grid optimization**, where smart meters in different households need to coordinate electricity consumption. As more smart meters join the system, computing an exact value decomposition for each agent becomes impractical. **Hierarchical reinforcement learning** and **graph neural networks** are often used to manage these scalability challenges.

Challenge 4: Function Approximation Errors in Deep MARL

Deep learning is often used to approximate value functions in complex MARL problems, but this introduces another challenge: **function approximation errors**. When training deep neural networks, small errors in Q-value estimation can compound over time, leading to **suboptimal policies**.

For example, in **multi-agent drone coordination**, if one drone's policy is based on **slightly incorrect Q-value approximations**, it may lead the entire fleet to an inefficient route. This is especially problematic in real-time applications where mistakes are costly.

To mitigate this, techniques such as **dueling networks, double Q-learning, and prioritized experience replay** are used to improve the accuracy of Q-value predictions.

Value decomposition is a powerful approach for training cooperative multi-agent systems, but it comes with major challenges. Assigning rewards fairly in a **dynamic, non-stationary** environment is difficult, and as more agents join the system, **scalability and function approximation errors** become serious concerns.

To address these issues, researchers use techniques such as **counterfactual credit assignment, QMIX for stability, centralized training with decentralized execution, and deep learning-based function approximation methods**.

As multi-agent AI becomes more widespread in **robotics, traffic control, and distributed AI systems**, improving value decomposition methods will be critical for building scalable and effective cooperative AI solutions.

5. Policy-Based and Actor-Critic Methods

Multi-Agent Reinforcement Learning (MARL) extends single-agent learning to environments where multiple agents **interact, adapt, and optimize decisions** while considering the actions of others. Traditional Q-learning and value-based methods, such as Deep Q-Networks (DQN), work well for discrete action spaces but **struggle in continuous action spaces** and highly dynamic environments.

This is where **policy-based methods** and **actor-critic methods** come into play. Instead of relying on a value function to decide actions, policy-based approaches directly **learn a mapping from states to actions**. Actor-critic methods **combine the best of both worlds** by using an actor (policy function) to select actions and a critic (value function) to evaluate them.

In multi-agent systems, these methods need additional refinements to handle **coordination, competition, and communication challenges**. This discussion will cover **Multi-Agent Deep Deterministic Policy Gradient (MADDPG), Proximal Policy Optimization (PPO) for multi-agent settings, and Trust Region Policy Optimization (TRPO)**, highlighting their strengths, weaknesses, real-world applications, and implementation techniques.

Multi-Agent Deep Deterministic Policy Gradient (MADDPG)

Multi-Agent Reinforcement Learning (MARL) presents unique challenges that do not exist in single-agent learning. When multiple agents interact in the same environment, their decisions influence not only the state of the world but also the learning process of other agents. This introduces problems such as **non-stationarity, coordination, competition, and credit assignment**.

Traditional Q-learning and value-based methods are not well suited for **continuous action spaces**, where agents must make precise adjustments rather than selecting from a discrete set of actions. **Deep Deterministic Policy Gradient (DDPG)** was designed to handle such cases, and **Multi-Agent**

DDPG (MADDPG) extends it to **multi-agent systems** by introducing a centralized learning mechanism while allowing decentralized execution.

Why Standard Q-Learning and DDPG Struggle in Multi-Agent Environments

Before diving into MADDPG, it's important to understand why standard Q-learning and DDPG face difficulties when applied to multi-agent systems.

Non-Stationarity of the Environment

In single-agent RL, the environment is assumed to be **stationary**—meaning that the agent's actions are the only source of change.

In MARL, each agent is learning **simultaneously**, making the environment constantly change. This violates the Markov property assumed by standard RL algorithms, leading to instability in learning.

Exploration Complexity

Each agent must not only explore **its own action space** but also account for how **other agents' actions** influence outcomes.

Simple exploration strategies, such as **epsilon-greedy**, do not work well in these environments because the reward landscape is highly dynamic.

Credit Assignment in Cooperative Tasks

If multiple agents contribute to achieving a shared reward, it becomes difficult to determine **which agent's actions were most responsible for success**.

Standard policy gradient methods update all agents equally, which can lead to **inefficient learning**.

Scalability in Large Agent Systems

As the number of agents increases, **the complexity of joint action spaces grows exponentially**.

A brute-force approach to modeling all agent interactions quickly becomes intractable.

How MADDPG Solves These Problems

MADDPG is an **actor-critic method** specifically designed for multi-agent learning in **continuous action spaces**. It improves upon standard DDPG by introducing **Centralized Training with Decentralized Execution (CTDE)**.

Centralized Training with Decentralized Execution (CTDE)

Each agent **maintains its own policy** but also has access to global information **during training**.

This allows agents to **learn coordinated strategies** while still making independent decisions during execution.

Multi-Agent Actor-Critic Framework

Each agent has:

An **Actor Network** that selects continuous actions.

A **Critic Network** that evaluates the joint actions of all agents.

This ensures that agents **learn to coordinate effectively** by considering the effects of all actions on the shared reward.

Handling Non-Stationarity with Shared Q-Functions

During training, each agent **updates its critic using the policies of all agents**, ensuring that it learns a stable representation of the environment.

This helps mitigate the **moving target problem** caused by other agents learning simultaneously.

Policy Gradient Optimization in Continuous Action Spaces

MADDPG optimizes policies using **deterministic policy gradients**, which are more sample-efficient than stochastic policy gradients.

The update equation for each agent's policy is:

$$\theta_i \leftarrow \theta_i + \alpha \nabla_{\theta_i} J(\theta_i)$$

The critic is trained using the Bellman equation:

$$Q_i(s, a_1, ..., a_N) = R + \gamma Q_i(s', \pi_1(s'), ..., \pi_N(s'))$$

The joint action-value function considers **the policies of all agents**, ensuring that the learned value function remains stable.

Real-World Applications of MADDPG

Autonomous Vehicle Coordination

Self-driving cars operate in **shared environments** where they must anticipate and react to the behavior of other vehicles. MADDPG is used to train fleets of **autonomous cars to navigate intersections, merge lanes, and avoid accidents** by considering other vehicles' decisions.

For example, if two autonomous cars approach a merging lane, one must decide to **slow down** while the other **accelerates** to avoid collision. MADDPG allows the agents to learn these **coordinated strategies** efficiently.

Multi-Robot Collaboration

In modern warehouses, **multiple robots must transport packages efficiently** without colliding or blocking pathways. MADDPG enables these robots to:

Learn how to **prioritize different tasks** based on package demand.

Coordinate movements **without explicit communication**.

Optimize **energy efficiency** by balancing workload distribution.

AI for Competitive Gaming

In strategy games like **Dota 2 or StarCraft II**, AI agents must compete while also forming temporary alliances. MADDPG helps:

Train AI teammates to **adapt to human players** in real-time.

Develop **opponent-aware policies** that counter different strategies.

Implementing MADDPG in Python

Let's implement a simple **MADDPG system** where two agents navigate a shared grid environment while avoiding collisions.

Step 1: Install Required Libraries

Ensure that you have TensorFlow installed:

```
pip install tensorflow numpy gym
```

Step 2: Define the MADDPG Agent

```python
import numpy as np
import tensorflow as tf
from tensorflow import keras

class MADDPGAgent:
    def __init__(self, state_size, action_size):
        self.actor = keras.Sequential([
            keras.layers.Dense(64,
activation='relu', input_shape=(state_size,)),
            keras.layers.Dense(64,
activation='relu'),
            keras.layers.Dense(action_size,
activation='tanh')  # Continuous action output
        ])

        self.critic = keras.Sequential([
            keras.layers.Dense(64,
activation='relu', input_shape=(state_size +
action_size,)),
            keras.layers.Dense(64,
activation='relu'),
            keras.layers.Dense(1,
activation='linear')
        ])


self.actor.compile(optimizer=keras.optimizers.Adam(
learning_rate=0.01))

self.critic.compile(optimizer=keras.optimizers.Adam
(learning_rate=0.01))

    def train(self, state, action, reward,
next_state):
        # Compute target value
        target_value = reward + 0.9 *
self.critic.predict(np.concatenate([next_state,
self.actor.predict(next_state)], axis=1))
        # Train critic
```

```
self.critic.train_on_batch(np.concatenate([state,
action], axis=1), target_value)
        # Train actor using policy gradient
        with tf.GradientTape() as tape:
            loss = -
tf.reduce_mean(self.critic(np.concatenate([state,
self.actor(state)], axis=1)))
        grads = tape.gradient(loss,
self.actor.trainable_variables)

        self.actor.optimizer.apply_gradients(zip(grads,
self.actor.trainable_variables))

# Create two agents
agent1 = MADDPGAgent(state_size=4, action_size=2)
agent2 = MADDPGAgent(state_size=4, action_size=2)
```

This code defines two **MADDPG agents**, each with a **policy network (actor)** and a **value network (critic)**. The agents are designed to learn in **continuous action spaces**, making them suitable for **robotics, self-driving cars, and complex cooperative AI environments**.

MADDPG provides a powerful way to **train multiple agents in continuous action spaces**, making it ideal for **cooperative and competitive multi-agent settings**. By leveraging **centralized training and decentralized execution**, MADDPG helps agents develop **stable, coordinated strategies** while maintaining independence during real-world execution.

As AI research progresses, MADDPG continues to play a vital role in **robotics, smart traffic systems, autonomous drones, and strategic decision-making AI**. Its ability to handle **complex, multi-agent interactions** makes it one of the most valuable reinforcement learning techniques available today.

Proximal Policy Optimization (PPO) for Multi-Agent Settings

Reinforcement learning (RL) in multi-agent settings is significantly more complex than in single-agent scenarios. In environments where multiple agents interact, the dynamics change constantly because every agent's decision affects the state of the environment, and consequently, the learning process of other agents. This creates issues like **non-stationarity, credit assignment, and coordination failure**.

Proximal Policy Optimization (PPO) has emerged as one of the most reliable policy-based reinforcement learning algorithms. It is widely used because of its **stability, sample efficiency, and ability to handle high-dimensional continuous action spaces**. In multi-agent settings, **PPO is extended to enable agents to learn cooperative or competitive strategies effectively** while maintaining stability in training.

Why PPO for Multi-Agent Reinforcement Learning?

Policy-based reinforcement learning is often preferred in MARL scenarios because **Q-learning and other value-based methods struggle with continuous action spaces and high-dimensional environments**.

PPO is particularly well-suited for MARL because:

It ensures stable policy updates.

Standard policy gradient methods suffer from **high variance**, leading to unstable learning. PPO introduces **clipping mechanisms** that prevent drastic updates, ensuring more consistent learning.

It allows agents to adapt without forgetting previous strategies.

In MARL, **other agents are also learning**, which makes the environment highly non-stationary. PPO's trust-region approach ensures that policies do not change too aggressively from one iteration to another, which helps in **avoiding catastrophic forgetting**.

It balances exploration and exploitation effectively.

In multi-agent settings, exploration is crucial because strategies depend on the behavior of other agents. PPO includes an **entropy bonus**, which encourages exploration when necessary.

It works well with decentralized and centralized training paradigms.

PPO can be used in **decentralized settings**, where each agent learns independently, or in **centralized training with decentralized execution (CTDE)**, where agents share information during training but act

How PPO Works in Multi-Agent Settings

PPO is an **actor-critic method**, meaning it maintains both a **policy function (actor)** that selects actions and a **value function (critic)** that evaluates those actions. This setup helps in reducing variance while still allowing direct optimization of the policy.

Policy Optimization with PPO

The core idea behind PPO is to **prevent drastic updates to the policy**, ensuring that the new policy does not deviate too far from the old one. It does this using a **clipped objective function**:

$$L(\theta) = \hat{E}_t \left[\min(r_t(\theta) A_t, \text{clip}(r_t(\theta), 1 - \epsilon, 1 + \epsilon) A_t) \right]$$

where:

$r_t(\theta) = \frac{\pi_{\theta}(a_t \mid s_t)}{\pi_{\theta_{\text{old}}}(a_t \mid s_t)}$ is the **probability ratio** between the new and old policy.

A_t is the **advantage function**, which estimates how much better an action was compared to the expected action.

ϵ is a **clipping parameter** that limits how much the new policy can differ from the old one.

The clipping function ensures that **policy updates are gradual**, preventing the model from making abrupt, suboptimal changes.

Multi-Agent PPO Training Strategy

In multi-agent settings, PPO can be implemented in **two primary ways**:

Independent PPO (Decentralized Learning):

Each agent learns its own policy independently.

The environment treats each agent separately, updating policies based on individual rewards.

Works well when **agents do not need to coordinate closely**.

Centralized Training with Decentralized Execution (CTDE):

Agents share some **global information during training** but make decisions independently during execution.

Useful for cooperative tasks, like **robot swarm coordination and traffic management**.

Real-World Applications of Multi-Agent PPO

Autonomous Traffic Signal Control

In modern cities, traffic congestion is a major issue. **Reinforcement learning-based traffic signal optimization** has shown promising results in improving traffic flow.

Each **traffic light** is treated as an agent.

Using **PPO with centralized training**, signals learn to **coordinate** with neighboring intersections to optimize traffic efficiency.

During execution, each light acts independently but follows learned cooperative policies.

Multi-Agent Drone Swarms

PPO is widely used in **drone fleet management**, where multiple UAVs must **cooperate to achieve a common objective** (e.g., area surveillance, package delivery).

PPO ensures that **drones learn coordinated movement patterns** while minimizing collision risks.

AI in Multiplayer Strategy Games

PPO has been successfully applied in **team-based competitive games like Dota 2**.

Each AI agent learns **individually but shares strategic information** during training to develop coordinated strategies.

Implementing Multi-Agent PPO in Python

We will implement **a simple multi-agent PPO system**, where two agents navigate a **grid environment** while learning optimal movement strategies.

Step 1: Install Dependencies

Ensure you have TensorFlow installed:

```
pip install tensorflow numpy gym
```

Step 2: Define the PPO Agent

```python
import numpy as np
import tensorflow as tf
from tensorflow import keras

class PPOAgent:
    def __init__(self, state_size, action_size):
        self.actor = keras.Sequential([
            keras.layers.Dense(64,
activation='relu', input_shape=(state_size,)),
            keras.layers.Dense(64,
activation='relu'),
            keras.layers.Dense(action_size,
activation='softmax')  # Probabilistic action
selection
        ])

        self.critic = keras.Sequential([
            keras.layers.Dense(64,
activation='relu', input_shape=(state_size,)),
```

```python
                keras.layers.Dense(64,
activation='relu'),
                keras.layers.Dense(1,
activation='linear')  # Value estimation
          ])


self.actor.compile(optimizer=keras.optimizers.Adam(
learning_rate=0.001),
loss='categorical_crossentropy')

self.critic.compile(optimizer=keras.optimizers.Adam
(learning_rate=0.001), loss='mse')

    def train(self, states, actions, advantages,
rewards):
        with tf.GradientTape() as tape:
            old_probs = self.actor(states)
            action_probs = tf.reduce_sum(old_probs
* actions, axis=1)
            ratios = action_probs / (old_probs +
1e-10)

            clipped_ratios =
tf.clip_by_value(ratios, 1 - 0.2, 1 + 0.2)
            loss = -
tf.reduce_mean(tf.minimum(ratios * advantages,
clipped_ratios * advantages))

        grads = tape.gradient(loss,
self.actor.trainable_variables)

self.actor.optimizer.apply_gradients(zip(grads,
self.actor.trainable_variables))

        self.critic.train_on_batch(states, rewards)

# Create two agents
agent1 = PPOAgent(state_size=4, action_size=2)
agent2 = PPOAgent(state_size=4, action_size=2)
```

PPO is one of the most powerful and **widely used** reinforcement learning algorithms for **multi-agent settings**. Its ability to **ensure stable updates, balance exploration, and handle continuous actions** makes it ideal for complex, dynamic environments.

In real-world applications, PPO has been successfully used in **autonomous traffic systems, robotic coordination, and AI-driven multiplayer gaming**. By leveraging **centralized training and decentralized execution**, it enables agents to learn cooperative strategies while still making independent decisions.

As AI-driven multi-agent systems become more advanced, PPO will continue to be a key tool in **teaching intelligent agents to collaborate, adapt, and optimize decisions in shared environments**.

Trust Region Policy Optimization (TRPO) and Its Applications

Reinforcement learning (RL) aims to teach agents to **make optimal decisions** by maximizing cumulative rewards in dynamic environments. In multi-agent reinforcement learning (MARL), this challenge becomes even more complex as multiple agents interact, **constantly changing the environment** for each other.

Policy gradient methods like **Proximal Policy Optimization (PPO) and Deep Deterministic Policy Gradient (DDPG)** have become popular for training agents in **continuous action spaces**, but they have limitations. PPO, for instance, introduces **clipping mechanisms** to stabilize learning, but it lacks the **strict theoretical guarantees** that prevent policies from making **dangerously large updates**.

Trust Region Policy Optimization (TRPO) is designed to solve this issue by ensuring that **policy updates remain within a trust region**, allowing stable and **more predictable policy improvements**. This is particularly useful in **multi-agent reinforcement learning**, where unpredictable updates can lead to chaotic behaviors, making it difficult for agents to learn optimal strategies.

Why TRPO?

Policy-based reinforcement learning methods like standard **policy gradient algorithms** update policies by computing the gradient of expected rewards and adjusting parameters in the direction of improvement. However, these methods can **take overly large steps**, leading to instability and suboptimal policies.

TRPO is designed to **keep policy updates within a "safe" region**, preventing drastic changes that could **reduce performance instead of improving it**.

How TRPO is Different from Other Policy Optimization Methods

Prevents Large Policy Updates

Instead of blindly applying the policy gradient update, TRPO **restricts updates** so that the new policy does not move too far from the previous one.

This is done using **Kullback-Leibler (KL) divergence**, a mathematical measure of how different two probability distributions are.

Theoretical Performance Guarantees

Unlike PPO, which uses an empirical clipping function, TRPO provides **strong theoretical guarantees** that ensure updates always **improve performance**.

More Efficient in Multi-Agent Systems

In **multi-agent reinforcement learning**, agents influence each other's learning.

TRPO ensures that updates are **gradual and predictable**, preventing situations where one agent's drastic change destabilizes the learning process of others.

How TRPO Works

TRPO optimizes policies using a constrained optimization approach. Instead of applying an **unrestricted gradient ascent**, TRPO **maximizes expected rewards while keeping the policy update within a trust region**.

Mathematical Formulation of TRPO

The goal is to find a new policy π_{θ} that maximizes expected rewards while keeping it within a certain distance of the previous policy $\pi_{\theta_{\text{old}}}$:

max⌊θ⌋θEπθold[πθ(a|s)πθold(a|s)Aπθold(s,a)]\max_{\theta} E_{\pi_{\theta_{\text{old}}}} \left[\frac{\pi_{\theta}(a|s)}{\pi_{\theta_{\text{old}}}(a|s)} A^{\pi_{\theta_{\text{old}}}}(s, a) \right]

Subject to a **KL-divergence constraint**:

DKL(πθ||πθold)≤δD_{\text{KL}}(\pi_{\theta} \| \pi_{\theta_{\text{old}}}) \leq \delta

where:

π_{θ}\pi_{\theta} is the new policy parameterized by θ\theta.

$\pi_{\theta_{old}}$\pi_{\theta_{\text{old}}} is the old policy.

Aπθold(s,a)A^{\pi_{\theta_{\text{old}}}}(s, a) is the **advantage function**, which measures how much better an action aa is compared to the expected outcome.

DKLD_{\text{KL}} is the **Kullback-Leibler divergence**, which ensures that the new policy does not deviate too much from the old policy.

δ\delta is the trust region size that limits how far the policy can change in one step.

By solving this **constrained optimization problem**, TRPO finds the best update while ensuring that the new policy is not drastically different from the previous one.

Real-World Applications of TRPO in Multi-Agent Learning

1. Multi-Agent Robot Coordination

TRPO is widely used in training **robot teams** for **search and rescue missions, warehouse management, and automated assembly lines**.

Robots must **coordinate their actions** while ensuring that small policy changes do not lead to **collisions or inefficiencies**.

TRPO helps by ensuring that policies improve **gradually and consistently**, preventing drastic shifts in movement patterns.

2. Autonomous Traffic Management

In modern cities, **intelligent traffic systems** must manage multiple intersections **cooperatively**.

Each traffic light is treated as an **independent agent**, but their actions must be **synchronized** for optimal traffic flow.

TRPO ensures that **policy updates do not cause sudden, counterproductive changes**, leading to **smoother traffic adaptation**.

3. AI for Competitive Games

TRPO is widely used in **multi-agent competitive games** like **poker, Dota 2, and StarCraft II**, where multiple AI agents compete and adapt to dynamic strategies.

Agents trained with TRPO **avoid making erratic moves** and learn **stable strategies** over time.

Implementing TRPO for Multi-Agent Learning

Let's implement **a simplified TRPO algorithm** for a multi-agent environment where two agents learn to navigate a grid **without colliding** while moving toward their respective goals.

Step 1: Install Dependencies

```
pip install tensorflow numpy gym
```

Step 2: Define the TRPO Agent

```python
import numpy as np
import tensorflow as tf
from tensorflow import keras

class TRPOAgent:
    def __init__(self, state_size, action_size):
        self.actor = keras.Sequential([
```

```python
            keras.layers.Dense(64,
activation='relu', input_shape=(state_size,)),
            keras.layers.Dense(64,
activation='relu'),
            keras.layers.Dense(action_size,
activation='softmax')  # Policy output
        ])

        self.critic = keras.Sequential([
            keras.layers.Dense(64,
activation='relu', input_shape=(state_size,)),
            keras.layers.Dense(64,
activation='relu'),
            keras.layers.Dense(1,
activation='linear')  # Value estimation
        ])


self.actor.compile(optimizer=keras.optimizers.Adam(
learning_rate=0.001),
loss='categorical_crossentropy')

self.critic.compile(optimizer=keras.optimizers.Adam
(learning_rate=0.001), loss='mse')

    def train(self, states, actions, advantages,
rewards, old_probs):
        with tf.GradientTape() as tape:
            new_probs = self.actor(states)
            ratio = tf.reduce_sum(new_probs *
actions, axis=1) / (old_probs + 1e-10)

            # KL divergence constraint
            kl_div = tf.reduce_mean(old_probs *
tf.math.log(old_probs / (new_probs + 1e-10)))
            if kl_div > 0.01:  # Trust region
threshold
                return  # Skip update if KL
divergence is too high

            loss = -tf.reduce_mean(ratio *
advantages)
```

```
        grads = tape.gradient(loss,
self.actor.trainable_variables)

self.actor.optimizer.apply_gradients(zip(grads,
self.actor.trainable_variables))

        self.critic.train_on_batch(states, rewards)
# Create two agents
agent1 = TRPOAgent(state_size=4, action_size=2)
agent2 = TRPOAgent(state_size=4, action_size=2)
```

Trust Region Policy Optimization (TRPO) is a **highly effective policy-based reinforcement learning algorithm** that provides **strong theoretical guarantees** for policy updates. Unlike standard policy gradient methods, TRPO **ensures stable, gradual improvements** without making abrupt, destabilizing changes.

In **multi-agent reinforcement learning**, TRPO is particularly valuable because it prevents agents from making large, **disruptive** updates that can negatively affect other agents. This makes it ideal for **robot coordination, traffic control, and competitive AI gaming**.

As multi-agent AI systems continue to evolve, **TRPO will remain a key algorithm for developing reliable and adaptable intelligent agents** that can operate in dynamic, high-stakes environments.

6. Communication and Coordination in MARL

Multi-Agent Reinforcement Learning (MARL) presents unique challenges that do not exist in single-agent environments. In a multi-agent system, **agents do not operate in isolation**—their actions influence not only the state of the environment but also the learning process of others. Because of this interdependence, **effective communication and coordination are essential** for agents to succeed in cooperative or mixed cooperative-competitive tasks.

Traditional reinforcement learning techniques often fail in these scenarios because they assume a static environment, while in MARL, the **environment itself is constantly changing** due to the simultaneous learning of multiple agents. To tackle this problem, researchers have developed **structured learning approaches** that enable agents to communicate, share useful information, and coordinate their actions effectively.

Centralized Training with Decentralized Execution (CTDE)

In multi-agent reinforcement learning (MARL), one of the biggest challenges is **how agents should learn and make decisions when interacting in a shared environment**. Unlike single-agent reinforcement learning, where an agent optimizes its policy based on a relatively static environment, MARL introduces **dynamic interdependencies**—meaning that each agent's decision affects the experiences of others.

This **non-stationarity** makes learning unstable, as agents must continuously adjust to changing behaviors. At the same time, agents in real-world applications—such as autonomous vehicles, robotic swarms, and financial trading algorithms—**cannot rely on constant communication during execution** due to bandwidth constraints, latency, or privacy concerns.

To address these challenges, the **Centralized Training with Decentralized Execution (CTDE)** paradigm has become a widely adopted solution. It allows agents to **leverage global information during training** while ensuring that their **policies remain decentralized** at execution time. This means that during real-world operation, agents can act independently without requiring direct access to other agents' observations or actions.

Why CTDE is Essential in Multi-Agent Systems

The core issue in MARL is that when multiple agents learn simultaneously, their **changing policies create a moving target**. This violates one of the basic assumptions of traditional reinforcement learning—that the environment is stationary.

CTDE addresses this by introducing a **structured approach** where:

During training, agents have access to **global state information** and the actions of other agents.

During execution, each agent acts **only based on its local observations** and learned policy.

This balance ensures that training is more efficient and effective while keeping execution scalable and practical for real-world deployment.

Example: Multi-Agent Autonomous Vehicles

Consider a network of **autonomous vehicles** that must navigate a dynamic urban environment while avoiding collisions and minimizing traffic congestion.

If each car **learns independently**, it may only optimize its own rewards without considering the impact on others, leading to **traffic bottlenecks or accidents**.

If cars can share data during **training**, they can learn how their decisions influence overall traffic flow.

However, during execution, each car **must make real-time decisions without waiting for communication** from others.

CTDE enables these vehicles to **learn coordinated strategies** during training while still **executing independently** on the road.

How CTDE Works

CTDE typically consists of:

A Centralized Critic (Value Function) for Training

Each agent has access to a **global critic** that evaluates its actions based on the complete environment state.

This critic helps agents **understand their impact on the system**, leading to better coordination.

Decentralized Actors for Execution

The **policy (actor)** of each agent is trained to **use only local observations** when making decisions.

This ensures that once deployed, each agent can act **autonomously** without requiring full system knowledge.

Mathematically, the **Q-value function** for an agent ii under CTDE is defined as:

$$Q_i(s, a_1, ..., a_N) = R + \gamma Q_i(s', \pi_1(s'), ..., \pi_N(s'))$$

where:

ss is the **global state** (available only during training).

$a_1, ..., a_N$ are the **actions of all agents**.

$\pi_i(s)$ is the **policy of agent ii**.

During **execution**, the policy $\pi_i(s)$ only uses **local observations**, making it **fully decentralized**.

CTDE in Different Learning Architectures

CTDE can be implemented using various learning frameworks, including:

1. Value-Based Methods (e.g., QMIX, VDN)

In these methods, the centralized critic learns a **joint Q-function** that combines the value functions of all agents.

The policy of each agent is optimized **based on this shared knowledge** during training but acts independently at execution.

Example: **QMIX** learns a **monotonic function** that ensures that individual Q-values contribute positively to the team objective.

2. Policy-Based Methods (e.g., MADDPG, COMA)

Here, each agent has an **actor (policy function)** that selects actions and a **centralized critic** that evaluates those actions.

This is particularly useful for **continuous action spaces**, such as robotics or drone fleets.

Example: **Multi-Agent Deep Deterministic Policy Gradient (MADDPG)** uses a centralized critic to learn **coordinated policies** while allowing agents to act independently in real-world tasks.

Real-World Applications of CTDE

1. Multi-Robot Warehouse Management

In modern warehouses (e.g., Amazon's fulfillment centers), hundreds of **automated robots** transport goods between storage and packaging stations.

If robots **operate without coordination**, they may create **traffic congestion** or inefficient routes.

Using **CTDE**, robots can **learn optimized strategies** during training but still function **independently** in execution.

This minimizes **communication overhead** while ensuring **optimal warehouse operations**.

2. Autonomous Drone Swarms

In disaster response or surveillance, drones must cover large areas **without colliding or overlapping coverage**.

During **training**, drones can share information to **learn cooperative strategies**.

During **execution**, each drone makes **real-time flight decisions** without waiting for global commands.

3. AI-Powered Financial Trading

Financial markets involve multiple autonomous **trading bots** that must make split-second decisions.

If each bot learns **independently**, it may not **account for market-wide trends**, leading to **inefficient trades**.

Using **CTDE**, bots can learn **market-aware strategies** during training but execute trades **independently** in real-time.

Implementing CTDE in Python

Let's build a **basic CTDE framework** using TensorFlow, where multiple agents learn **coordinated strategies** but act **independently** during execution.

Step 1: Install Dependencies

```
pip install tensorflow numpy gym
```

Step 2: Define the CTDE Agent

```python
import numpy as np
import tensorflow as tf
from tensorflow import keras

class CTDEAgent:
    def __init__(self, state_size, action_size):
        self.actor = keras.Sequential([
            keras.layers.Dense(64,
activation='relu', input_shape=(state_size,)),
            keras.layers.Dense(64,
activation='relu'),
            keras.layers.Dense(action_size,
activation='softmax')  # Policy output
        ])

        self.critic = keras.Sequential([
```

```python
              keras.layers.Dense(64,
activation='relu', input_shape=(state_size * 2,)),
# Uses global state
              keras.layers.Dense(64,
activation='relu'),
              keras.layers.Dense(1,
activation='linear')  # Centralized value function
         ])


self.actor.compile(optimizer=keras.optimizers.Adam(
learning_rate=0.001),
loss='categorical_crossentropy')

self.critic.compile(optimizer=keras.optimizers.Adam
(learning_rate=0.001), loss='mse')

    def train(self, local_states, global_states,
actions, rewards):
        with tf.GradientTape() as tape:
            new_probs = self.actor(local_states)
            action_probs = tf.reduce_sum(new_probs
* actions, axis=1)
            loss = -tf.reduce_mean(action_probs *
rewards)  # Policy gradient loss

        grads = tape.gradient(loss,
self.actor.trainable_variables)

self.actor.optimizer.apply_gradients(zip(grads,
self.actor.trainable_variables))

        self.critic.train_on_batch(global_states,
rewards)

# Create two agents
agent1 = CTDEAgent(state_size=4, action_size=2)
agent2 = CTDEAgent(state_size=4, action_size=2)
```

CTDE is a powerful paradigm that enables **scalable, efficient multi-agent learning** by combining **the advantages of centralized training and decentralized execution**.

It **reduces non-stationarity** by using shared information during training.

It **ensures scalability** by allowing agents to act independently at execution.

It **improves coordination** in multi-agent tasks such as **robotics, autonomous driving, and financial markets**.

As MARL continues to evolve, **CTDE will remain a foundational approach for training intelligent, autonomous multi-agent systems**.

Graph Neural Networks (GNNs) for Agent Communication

In multi-agent reinforcement learning (MARL), agents operate in **dynamic, partially observable environments** where effective decision-making depends on both **local observations** and **communication with other agents**. Unlike single-agent reinforcement learning, where an agent learns based on a stable environment, MARL requires agents to continuously **adapt to the behaviors of other learning entities**.

For example, in **robotic swarm coordination, autonomous traffic management, and multiplayer strategy games**, agents must **exchange information** to achieve shared objectives efficiently. However, the challenge is that **direct communication can be expensive, unreliable, or even infeasible** in real-world applications.

This is where **Graph Neural Networks (GNNs)** come into play. GNNs provide a structured way to model agent interactions, allowing agents to **share relevant information efficiently** without requiring explicit global communication. This enables **better coordination, improved decision-making, and faster learning** in complex multi-agent environments.

Why Traditional Communication Methods Fail in MARL

In traditional MARL, agents often rely on **explicit message-passing mechanisms** to share information. However, this approach has several limitations:

Scalability Issues

If every agent communicates with every other agent, the communication overhead increases **exponentially** as the number of agents grows.

Redundant or Irrelevant Information

Agents may receive **too much data**, making it difficult to extract useful signals while ignoring noise.

Latency and Bandwidth Constraints

In **real-time applications** such as autonomous vehicle networks, drones, and financial trading systems, constant communication introduces **delays** that make decisions outdated.

Single Point of Failure

If agents rely on a **centralized communication system**, failures in the system can cause **breakdowns in coordination**.

To overcome these challenges, GNNs allow agents to **learn implicit communication strategies** by structuring agent interactions as a **graph**, where only the most relevant information is exchanged.

How Graph Neural Networks (GNNs) Enable Agent Communication

GNNs are designed to process data that is structured as a **graph**. In the context of MARL, the **agents** act as **nodes**, and their communication links define the **edges** of the graph.

Each agent receives information from its **neighboring agents**, aggregates it, and updates its internal representation before making a decision.

Mathematical Representation of GNNs for MARL

Each agent ii has a **state representation** h_i, which is updated based on information from its neighbors:

$$h_i^{(t+1)} = \sigma\left(W_1 h_i^{(t)} + W_2 \sum_{j \in \mathcal{N}(i)} h_j^{(t)} \right)$$

where:

$h_i^{(t)}$ represents the agent's internal representation at time step t.

$\mathcal{N}(i)$ denotes the neighboring agents of i.

W_1 and W_2 are learnable weight matrices.

σ is an activation function (e.g., ReLU).

This equation shows that each agent **updates its state based on its own knowledge and the aggregated information from its neighbors**.

How GNNs Improve MARL Communication

Selective Communication

Instead of sharing all information, agents **learn which neighbors are important** and selectively exchange information.

Distributed and Scalable

Unlike centralized approaches, GNN-based communication **scales efficiently** as the number of agents increases.

Implicit Coordination

Agents learn to **communicate only when necessary**, reducing communication overhead.

Real-World Applications of GNNs in Multi-Agent Systems

1. Multi-Agent Traffic Signal Optimization

In large cities, **traffic lights must be optimized dynamically** to reduce congestion. Each traffic light acts as an **agent**, and its decision affects nearby intersections.

Using a **GNN-based MARL system**, traffic lights share only **relevant data** with neighboring intersections.

This allows them to learn **when to extend or shorten signal times** based on real-time traffic conditions.

The system leads to **faster adaptation to traffic patterns** and improved overall efficiency.

2. Swarm Robotics for Search and Rescue

In disaster response, **autonomous robots must navigate collapsed buildings** to locate survivors. These robots:

Have **limited visibility** due to debris and obstacles.

Must **exchange local information** to **build a shared understanding** of the environment.

Use GNNs to ensure that **only the most relevant navigation data** is shared, reducing communication overhead.

This approach ensures that rescue robots **explore the environment efficiently** while avoiding redundant searches.

3. AI Coordination in Multiplayer Games

GNNs are widely used in **multi-agent AI for strategic team-based games**, such as:

Dota 2 and StarCraft II, where AI teammates must coordinate attacks and defenses.

Cooperative AI bots in FPS games, where GNNs help agents share tactical information (e.g., enemy positions, safe zones).

By structuring communication as a **graph**, AI teammates learn **how to cooperate more effectively** in real time.

Implementing GNN-Based Communication in Python

Let's implement a **simple GNN-based communication system** for agents navigating a shared environment.

Step 1: Install Dependencies

```
pip install tensorflow numpy networkx gym
```

Step 2: Define the GNN Model

```python
import numpy as np
import tensorflow as tf
import networkx as nx
from tensorflow import keras

class GNNLayer(keras.layers.Layer):
    def __init__(self, output_dim):
        super(GNNLayer, self).__init__()
        self.output_dim = output_dim
        self.dense = keras.layers.Dense(output_dim,
activation='relu')

    def call(self, node_features,
adjacency_matrix):
        neighbor_features =
tf.matmul(adjacency_matrix, node_features)   #
Aggregate neighbors
        combined_features =
tf.concat([node_features, neighbor_features],
axis=-1)
        return self.dense(combined_features)

class MultiAgentGNN(keras.Model):
    def __init__(self, num_agents, feature_size,
output_dim):
        super(MultiAgentGNN, self).__init__()
        self.gnn_layer = GNNLayer(output_dim)
        self.policy_head =
keras.layers.Dense(output_dim,
activation='softmax')

    def call(self, states, adjacency_matrix):
        agent_features = self.gnn_layer(states,
adjacency_matrix)
        return self.policy_head(agent_features)

# Define a simple adjacency matrix for 3 agents
adjacency_matrix = np.array([[1, 1, 0],
                             [1, 1, 1],
                             [0, 1, 1]],
dtype=np.float32)
```

```
# Initialize agent states (randomized)
agent_states = np.random.rand(3, 4)

# Create and test the GNN model
gnn_model = MultiAgentGNN(num_agents=3,
feature_size=4, output_dim=2)
output_actions = gnn_model(agent_states,
adjacency_matrix)
print("Action probabilities:",
output_actions.numpy())
```

How This Works

Each agent **aggregates information from neighboring agents** based on the **adjacency matrix**.

The **GNN layer processes this information** and outputs a **policy distribution** for each agent.

The model ensures that agents learn **to communicate effectively**, rather than sharing **all information blindly**.

GNNs provide a powerful way for **agents to communicate selectively and coordinate their actions** without relying on centralized control. This makes them ideal for **scalable, decentralized multi-agent systems** in real-world applications such as **robotics, smart cities, and AI-driven multiplayer games**.

They reduce communication overhead by ensuring that agents only exchange **useful information**.

They improve coordination by structuring agents as a **graph-based network**.

They scale efficiently, making them suitable for environments with **large numbers of interacting agents**.

As MARL research continues to evolve, **GNN-based communication will play a crucial role in enabling next-generation AI systems** that can function collaboratively in complex, real-world environments.

Emergent Cooperation and Coordination Strategies

In **Multi-Agent Reinforcement Learning (MARL)**, one of the most fascinating phenomena is the emergence of **cooperation and coordination** among agents—even when no explicit cooperation mechanism is enforced. Unlike single-agent reinforcement learning, where the focus is solely on maximizing individual rewards, multi-agent environments require agents to **consider the actions of others** to achieve long-term success.

The challenge, however, is that **cooperation and coordination are not always pre-programmed**. Instead, they often **emerge naturally** through the interactions of learning agents. In many cases, agents discover that working together can be more beneficial than acting purely in self-interest.

Why Cooperation and Coordination Matter in MARL

In many real-world scenarios, multiple autonomous systems must work together to **optimize group performance**. Examples include:

Autonomous Vehicles: Cars in traffic must coordinate lane changes, speed adjustments, and merging behavior to avoid congestion and collisions.

Robot Swarms: Groups of robots in warehouses or search-and-rescue missions must share tasks efficiently without central control.

Multi-Agent Finance: Trading algorithms in financial markets must learn to react to market changes while ensuring they do not negatively impact overall liquidity.

AI in Team-Based Games: In multiplayer video games, AI-controlled teammates must learn to assist human players rather than playing selfishly.

In these settings, **purely independent learning** often leads to **suboptimal outcomes**, as each agent focuses only on short-term rewards. Effective cooperation emerges when agents recognize the **long-term benefits of teamwork**.

How Does Cooperation Emerge in MARL?

1. Learning Through Shared Rewards

One of the simplest ways to encourage cooperation is through **reward shaping**—modifying the reward function to reflect shared goals. If agents receive **individual rewards**, they might act selfishly. However, if they receive **a collective reward**, they learn that **helping others benefits them as well**.

For example, in **multi-agent traffic signal optimization**, each traffic light can be rewarded based on **overall traffic flow efficiency** rather than just minimizing its own wait time. This encourages **coordination** between intersections to prevent bottlenecks.

Mathematically, if R_i is the reward for agent i, we modify it to a **shared reward function**:

$$R_i = \sum_{j=1}^{N} R_j$$

where N is the total number of agents. This ensures that each agent considers the impact of its actions on the group.

2. Implicit Coordination Through Experience

Even when rewards are **individual**, cooperation can still emerge **naturally** as agents learn **how their actions impact the overall environment**. This is particularly common in environments where:

Agents must interact repeatedly over many time steps.

Selfish behavior leads to negative long-term consequences.

Competition forces agents to recognize the value of alliances.

For example, in **multi-agent soccer**, an AI agent may initially try to **score goals alone**. However, as it experiences **frequent ball losses**, it learns that **passing to a teammate increases overall chances of scoring**—even if it does not directly control the final shot.

This behavior arises through **trial and error**, where **successful patterns of teamwork are reinforced over time**.

3. Multi-Agent Credit Assignment and Counterfactual Learning

One challenge in cooperative MARL is **credit assignment**—determining **which agent's actions contributed to success or failure**. If agents cannot tell whether their **cooperation mattered**, they will struggle to reinforce positive behaviors.

A **counterfactual baseline** helps address this by estimating **what would have happened if an agent had acted differently**.

For example, in **a cooperative drone delivery system**, if one drone **waits to let another pass**, how do we measure whether that action **helped optimize deliveries**?

We use a **counterfactual Q-function** that compares actual performance with a **hypothetical scenario where the agent had taken a different action**:

$Q(s,a) - Q(s,a')Q(s, a) - Q(s, a')$

This helps agents learn which **cooperative behaviors truly made a difference**.

4. Emergent Communication Without Explicit Messages

Agents often **develop their own ways of signaling intent** without explicit communication channels. In **multi-agent reinforcement learning**, this is known as **emergent communication**.

For example, in **cooperative robot path planning**, robots may learn to adjust their movement patterns in subtle ways—such as **slowing down slightly**—to indicate to others that they should pass first.

This is achieved through **policy learning**, where reinforcement learning algorithms optimize **not only what actions to take but also how to make those actions interpretable to others**.

Real-World Applications of Emergent Cooperation in MARL

Autonomous Traffic Control

A classic example of emergent cooperation is seen in **multi-agent traffic signal control**.

Instead of controlling lights independently, agents learn to **observe congestion patterns** and adapt signals dynamically.

Over time, they develop **self-organizing behavior** where certain lights hold green signals longer to **clear major roads**, reducing overall congestion.

Swarm Robotics for Exploration

In search-and-rescue operations, a fleet of autonomous robots must **explore unknown terrain** efficiently.

With **independent learning**, they might explore **redundant areas**, wasting time.

With **emergent cooperation**, robots **adjust their search patterns** based on their peers' movements, leading to **faster coverage of an area**.

AI Teammates in Competitive Video Games

AI agents in team-based games like **Dota 2 and StarCraft II** must develop strategies that balance **offense, defense, and resource sharing**.

Through **trial and reinforcement**, AI teammates learn to **support human players**, assisting in battles and distributing resources efficiently.

Implementing Emergent Cooperation in a Multi-Agent Grid Environment

Let's build a simple MARL system where two agents learn to **cooperate to reach a shared goal**.

Step 1: Install Dependencies

```
pip install tensorflow numpy gym
```

Step 2: Define the Environment

```python
import numpy as np
import random

class MultiAgentGrid:
    def __init__(self, grid_size=5, goal=(4, 4)):
        self.grid_size = grid_size
```

```
        self.goal = goal
        self.agent_positions = [(0, 0), (0, 1)]   #
Initial positions

    def step(self, actions):
        new_positions = []
        for i, (x, y) in
enumerate(self.agent_positions):
            if actions[i] == "up":
                x = max(0, x - 1)
            elif actions[i] == "down":
                x = min(self.grid_size - 1, x + 1)
            elif actions[i] == "left":
                y = max(0, y - 1)
            elif actions[i] == "right":
                y = min(self.grid_size - 1, y + 1)
            new_positions.append((x, y))

        # Reward agents if both reach goal
        reward = 10 if new_positions[0] ==
self.goal and new_positions[1] == self.goal else -1
        self.agent_positions = new_positions
        return self.agent_positions, reward
```

Step 3: Training with Shared Rewards

```
class RLAgent:
    def __init__(self):
        self.q_table = np.zeros((5, 5, 4))   #
Simple Q-learning table
        self.lr = 0.1
        self.gamma = 0.9

    def select_action(self, state):
        return np.argmax(self.q_table[state[0],
state[1]])

    def update(self, state, action, reward,
next_state):
        best_next_action =
np.max(self.q_table[next_state[0], next_state[1]])
```

```
        self.q_table[state[0], state[1], action] +=
self.lr * (reward + self.gamma * best_next_action -
self.q_table[state[0], state[1], action])

agent1, agent2 = RLAgent(), RLAgent()
```

This simple **cooperative Q-learning** setup encourages agents to learn **shared strategies**, leading to **emergent cooperation** over time.

Emergent cooperation in MARL **is not pre-programmed—it arises naturally** when agents discover that **helping others also helps themselves**. Through **shared rewards, implicit coordination, and communication strategies**, agents in multi-agent environments can **develop complex cooperative behaviors** that optimize group performance.

As AI research advances, these methods will play a critical role in **smart traffic systems, robotics, financial trading, and next-generation AI teammates in games**.

7. Scalability and Stability in MARL

Multi-Agent Reinforcement Learning (MARL) is a powerful framework that enables multiple autonomous agents to **learn, interact, and adapt** in complex environments. However, as the number of agents increases, MARL systems face **severe scalability and stability challenges**.

Unlike single-agent reinforcement learning, where an agent only needs to learn optimal strategies in a relatively stable environment, MARL introduces:

Exponential growth in state-action spaces, making learning increasingly difficult.

Non-stationarity, as each agent's learning process continuously alters the environment.

Credit assignment difficulties, where it becomes unclear which agent's actions contributed to success or failure.

This chapter will explore:

The curse of dimensionality in multi-agent settings and how it affects scalability.

Reward shaping and credit assignment techniques to improve stability.

How meta-learning helps agents generalize across different multi-agent environments.

Each of these areas plays a crucial role in making MARL **scalable, efficient, and stable** in real-world applications.

The Curse of Dimensionality in Multi-Agent Settings

As multi-agent reinforcement learning (MARL) is applied to more complex environments, a major challenge arises: **the curse of dimensionality**. This refers to the exponential growth of computational complexity as the number of agents, states, and actions increases.

In single-agent reinforcement learning, an agent interacts with an environment and learns an optimal policy by mapping states to actions. However, in a multi-agent setting, each agent's decisions depend on the actions of other agents, significantly increasing the size of the state-action space. This growth makes learning difficult, slows down convergence, and limits the scalability of MARL algorithms.

Understanding the Curse of Dimensionality

How State and Action Spaces Grow in MARL

In a single-agent system with:

SS possible states

AA possible actions

The Q-table (used in Q-learning) has a size of:

$Q(S,A)Q(S, A)$

For a **multi-agent system** with NN agents, where each agent has:

SS possible states

AA possible actions

The **joint state space** grows as:

SNS^N

And the **joint action space** grows as:

ANA^N

This means the Q-table must store values for **every possible combination of states and actions across all agents**, making the learning process exponentially harder.

For example:

Number of Agents State Space Action Space Q-Table Size

Number of Agents	State Space	Action Space	Q-Table Size
1 Agent	100	10	1,000

Number of Agents	State Space	Action Space	Q-Table Size
2 Agents	10,000	100	1,000,000
3 Agents	1,000,000	1,000	1,000,000,000

At just **three agents**, the number of possible state-action combinations reaches one billion, making it **impractical to store or compute**.

Why Large State-Action Spaces Cause Problems

Increased Computational Complexity

Traditional reinforcement learning methods like Q-learning rely on **tabular representations**, which become infeasible as state-action spaces grow.

Even deep reinforcement learning methods struggle because larger state spaces require **more training data and computational resources**.

Slower Learning and Convergence

As the number of agents increases, algorithms require **more training episodes** to explore and learn effective policies.

This significantly **slows down** convergence, meaning agents take longer to develop optimal behaviors.

Non-Stationarity in Multi-Agent Learning

Since multiple agents are learning at the same time, the environment **keeps changing** dynamically.

This makes it difficult for any individual agent to learn a **stable policy**, as what works in one episode might fail in the next.

Exploration vs. Exploitation Becomes Harder

In single-agent reinforcement learning, exploration helps the agent discover **better actions**.

In MARL, the **number of possible actions grows exponentially**, making it harder to explore all potential strategies efficiently.

Strategies to Mitigate the Curse of Dimensionality

Despite these challenges, several techniques help make MARL **more scalable and computationally feasible**.

1. Factored or Approximate Value Functions

Instead of storing a full Q-table, reinforcement learning algorithms can use **function approximation** techniques such as:

Deep Q-Networks (DQN): Uses neural networks to approximate Q-values, allowing learning in high-dimensional state spaces.

Value Decomposition Networks (VDN): Decomposes the global Q-function into individual agent Q-functions, making multi-agent learning more efficient.

These methods significantly **reduce memory and computation requirements** while still allowing agents to learn optimal policies.

2. Centralized Training with Decentralized Execution (CTDE)

CTDE is a popular approach where:

Training is centralized, meaning agents have access to a shared critic function that considers the global state and actions of all agents.

Execution is decentralized, meaning each agent makes decisions independently using only its own local observations.

This approach **reduces the effective action space** at execution time while still leveraging shared knowledge during training.

Example: **Multi-Agent Deep Deterministic Policy Gradient (MADDPG)**

MADDPG uses **centralized critics** that receive global state information during training but allows agents to act **independently during execution**.

3. Multi-Agent Attention Mechanisms

In environments where many agents interact, **not all agents are relevant to every decision**. Instead of considering **all agents at once**, MARL can use **attention mechanisms** to focus only on **important agents** in a given scenario.

Graph Neural Networks (GNNs): Model agents as nodes in a graph, allowing efficient message-passing between only relevant agents.

Attention-based MARL: Agents selectively **focus on teammates or competitors** that impact their decisions the most, reducing complexity.

This helps scale MARL to larger environments where **hundreds of agents** must coordinate without needing full state-space representation.

4. Parameter Sharing and Transfer Learning

Instead of training each agent separately, MARL can **share neural network parameters** among agents to improve learning efficiency.

Homogeneous Agent Training: If multiple agents share the same role, they can **learn from the same policy network**, reducing the number of independent learning processes.

Transfer Learning in MARL: Agents trained in one environment can **transfer knowledge** to a new environment, reducing the need for retraining from scratch.

Example: **In warehouse robots**, different robots performing the same task can **use a shared policy**, significantly reducing training time.

5. Hierarchical Reinforcement Learning (HRL) for Multi-Agent Systems

Hierarchical reinforcement learning introduces **multiple levels of decision-making**:

High-level policies dictate broad strategies (e.g., "prioritize safety over speed").

Low-level policies handle specific tasks (e.g., "adjust speed based on the distance to the next agent").

This hierarchical approach **reduces the effective decision space**, making MARL more scalable.

Example: **Autonomous Driving**

A **high-level policy** determines when to yield at intersections.

A **low-level policy** controls steering and acceleration.

By breaking down tasks, MARL algorithms **avoid unnecessary complexity** while maintaining high performance.

The curse of dimensionality is one of the biggest challenges in MARL, making learning **slower, less efficient, and computationally expensive** as the number of agents increases. However, several strategies can help:

Using function approximation (Deep Q-Networks, VDN) instead of full Q-tables

Centralized Training with Decentralized Execution (CTDE) to share knowledge efficiently

Attention mechanisms and Graph Neural Networks (GNNs) to limit unnecessary interactions

Parameter sharing and transfer learning to accelerate training

Hierarchical Reinforcement Learning (HRL) to decompose complex tasks

By applying these techniques, MARL can scale to real-world applications such as **autonomous traffic systems, multi-robot collaboration, and AI-driven financial markets**—enabling intelligent agents to learn and interact efficiently even in high-dimensional environments.

Reward Shaping and Credit Assignment Solutions

In multi-agent reinforcement learning (MARL), agents interact with an environment, learning strategies that maximize rewards through trial and error. However, in multi-agent settings, assigning appropriate rewards to each agent is not straightforward. Since multiple agents contribute to the same outcomes, it becomes difficult to determine which actions were responsible for success or failure.

This problem is known as the **credit assignment problem**—a challenge that can prevent agents from learning effective cooperative behaviors. Without proper credit assignment, agents may receive **misleading rewards**, leading to suboptimal or even counterproductive strategies.

To overcome this, **reward shaping** is used to guide agents toward desirable behaviors by modifying the reward function. By structuring rewards carefully, agents can **learn faster, coordinate better, and avoid unintended behaviors**.

Why Credit Assignment is Difficult in Multi-Agent Systems

In a single-agent system, credit assignment is relatively simple. An agent takes an action, observes a result, and updates its strategy accordingly.

In MARL, however, multiple agents contribute to a shared outcome. If a team of agents achieves a goal, **who gets credit for the success?**

For example, in a **robotic warehouse**, if a package is delivered successfully, was it because:

One robot found the shortest route?

Another robot moved out of the way to prevent congestion?

A third robot communicated the correct path?

Without proper credit assignment, agents may:

Overestimate or underestimate their contributions

Fail to recognize the true cause of success

Develop selfish behaviors instead of cooperating

To address this, reward shaping and credit assignment solutions are necessary.

Reward Shaping: Guiding Agents Toward Efficient Learning

Reward shaping is the process of **modifying the reward function** to guide agents toward better strategies. Instead of relying solely on sparse or delayed rewards, agents receive **additional feedback** to help them learn faster.

Mathematically, if the original reward function is $R(s,a)R(s, a)$, reward shaping introduces an additional term $F(s,a)F(s, a)$, creating a **new reward function**:

$R'(s,a)=R(s,a)+F(s,a)R'(s, a) = R(s, a) + F(s, a)$

where:

$R(s,a)R(s, a)$ is the original reward.

$F(s,a)F(s, a)$ is the shaping function that provides **additional guidance**.

Types of Reward Shaping

Potential-Based Reward Shaping (PBRS)

PBRS ensures that reward modifications do not **change the optimal policy**, only accelerate learning.

A potential function $\Phi(s)\backslash Phi(s)$ defines the desirability of a state:

$F(s,a)=\gamma\Phi(s')-\Phi(s)F(s, a) = \gamma \Phi(s') - \Phi(s)$

Example: In a **multi-agent rescue mission**, if a drone is moving toward a fire, $\Phi(s)\backslash Phi(s)$ could be **higher in areas near the fire**, guiding it in the right direction.

Dense Reward Shaping

Instead of rewarding only **final outcomes**, intermediate progress is rewarded.

Example: In **multi-agent soccer**, agents can be rewarded not only for **scoring a goal** but also for **successful passes**.

Shaping Through Demonstration

A human expert or a trained policy provides **example actions**, and rewards are shaped based on similarity.

Example: In **cooperative drone flight**, an expert trajectory could be used to guide drones toward optimal formations.

Credit Assignment Solutions: Ensuring Fair Reward Distribution

1. Global Rewards with Counterfactual Baselines

One simple approach is to give **all agents the same global reward** based on team success. However, this does not tell each agent how **important its contribution** was.

To solve this, counterfactual baselines estimate **what would have happened if an agent had acted differently**.

If the team receives reward R, and removing agent i leads to reward R_{-i}, then the **true impact** of the agent's action is:

$$\Delta R_i = R - R_{-i}$$

If removing an agent **significantly decreases** the reward, it is **given more credit**.

Example: In **cooperative warehouse robots**, if disabling a robot increases delivery time, it means that robot **was contributing positively**, and it should be rewarded accordingly.

2. Difference Rewards (D)

The **difference reward method** helps agents measure their **real impact** on the system.

Instead of giving a global reward R, each agent receives:

$$D_i = R - R_{-i}$$

This tells the agent **how much better (or worse) the team performed because of its actions**.

Example: In **multi-agent drone formations**, a drone's reward is based on **how much its movement helped the formation** compared to if it had stayed still.

3. Individual Shaped Rewards for Coordination

Sometimes, assigning global rewards is not enough, and agents need **individual incentives** to cooperate.

Example: In **multi-agent self-driving cars**, reward shaping can encourage:

Smooth merging into lanes instead of cutting in aggressively.

Reducing braking frequency to improve traffic flow.

By giving **small rewards for cooperative behaviors**, agents learn **how to act efficiently in shared spaces**.

Real-World Applications of Reward Shaping and Credit Assignment

1. Multi-Agent Traffic Control

Without proper credit assignment, each intersection may optimize its own traffic light timing **without considering the impact on nearby roads**.

By using counterfactual rewards, traffic systems **learn that synchronizing signals leads to reduced congestion**.

2. Cooperative AI in Video Games

In **team-based multiplayer games**, agents must **learn to pass, assist, and defend effectively**.

Reward shaping ensures AI agents **do not only chase individual achievements but work toward team success**.

3. Multi-Robot Task Allocation

In warehouse automation, robots must **coordinate to transport packages** efficiently.

Credit assignment ensures robots that **prioritize urgent tasks** receive better rewards than those who take random paths.

Implementing Reward Shaping in a Multi-Agent Gridworld

Let's create a **Python simulation** where agents must cooperate to reach a shared goal.

Step 1: Install Dependencies

```
pip install tensorflow numpy gym
```

Step 2: Define the Multi-Agent Grid Environment

```
import numpy as np
```

```python
class MultiAgentGrid:
    def __init__(self, grid_size=5, goal=(4, 4)):
        self.grid_size = grid_size
        self.goal = goal
        self.agent_positions = [(0, 0), (0, 1)]  #
Initial positions

    def step(self, actions):
        new_positions = []
        for i, (x, y) in
enumerate(self.agent_positions):
            if actions[i] == "up":
                x = max(0, x - 1)
            elif actions[i] == "down":
                x = min(self.grid_size - 1, x + 1)
            elif actions[i] == "left":
                y = max(0, y - 1)
            elif actions[i] == "right":
                y = min(self.grid_size - 1, y + 1)
            new_positions.append((x, y))

        reward = -1
        if new_positions[0] == self.goal and
new_positions[1] == self.goal:
            reward = 10  # Team reward for
cooperation

        self.agent_positions = new_positions
        return self.agent_positions, reward
```

Step 3: Training with Reward Shaping

```python
class RLAgent:
    def __init__(self):
        self.q_table = np.zeros((5, 5, 4))

    def select_action(self, state):
        return np.argmax(self.q_table[state[0],
state[1]])

    def update(self, state, action, reward,
next_state):
```

```
        best_next_action =
np.max(self.q_table[next_state[0], next_state[1]])
        self.q_table[state[0], state[1], action] +=
0.1 * (reward + 0.9 * best_next_action -
self.q_table[state[0], state[1], action])
```

This method **encourages cooperation** by giving agents **shared rewards for reaching the goal together**.

Reward shaping and credit assignment are essential for **stabilizing MARL systems, improving cooperation, and ensuring efficient learning**. Without them, agents may develop **selfish or inefficient behaviors**. By applying these techniques, MARL can scale effectively to **robotics, smart traffic systems, and cooperative AI applications**.

Meta-Learning for Scalable MARL

Multi-Agent Reinforcement Learning (MARL) enables multiple autonomous agents to learn and adapt in complex environments. However, as the number of agents increases, training becomes significantly more **computationally expensive and less stable**. Agents must not only learn how to optimize their own actions but also adapt to the behaviors of others.

This scaling problem is one of the biggest barriers to applying MARL in **real-world applications**, such as **robotic swarms, traffic management, autonomous drone fleets, and large-scale economic simulations**.

Meta-learning—often referred to as **learning to learn**—provides a powerful way to improve MARL scalability. Instead of training agents from scratch every time they encounter a new environment, meta-learning teaches them **how to adapt quickly based on past experiences**. This allows agents to generalize across different multi-agent scenarios, significantly reducing training time while improving coordination.

Why Scalability is a Major Challenge in MARL

1. Large State-Action Spaces

In a single-agent setting, the agent needs to explore and learn from a state space of size SS and an action space of size AA.

For a multi-agent system with NN agents, the total **joint state space** becomes:

SNS^N

And the **joint action space** grows as:

ANA^N

This exponential growth makes learning **much slower** as more agents are added, leading to **longer convergence times** and inefficient coordination.

2. Non-Stationarity in Multi-Agent Learning

In MARL, agents are learning simultaneously, **constantly changing the environment** for each other. This means:

An optimal policy in one episode may no longer be effective in the next.

The reward landscape shifts dynamically, making it hard for agents to converge to stable strategies.

3. Lack of Generalization Across Tasks

If an agent has learned a strategy in one environment, it **cannot easily transfer that knowledge** to a new environment.

This forces agents to **retrain from scratch** every time they face a new scenario, **wasting computational resources**.

How Meta-Learning Solves Scalability Challenges

Meta-learning provides a way to **train agents on a distribution of tasks**, so that they learn how to **adapt efficiently** when faced with new tasks. Instead of learning individual policies, agents learn **meta-policies** that enable them to generalize and adapt quickly.

A meta-learning agent does not just learn **what to do** but also learns **how to learn**—allowing it to adjust its strategy dynamically based on **past experiences**.

The Meta-Learning Process

Meta-learning typically consists of **two phases**:

Meta-Training Phase:

The agent is trained across a variety of MARL tasks.

The goal is to find a model that can **quickly adapt** to unseen scenarios.

Adaptation Phase:

When introduced to a new MARL task, the agent **adapts with minimal training data** instead of starting from scratch.

Mathematically, meta-learning optimizes policies to minimize the **expected loss over multiple tasks**:

$$\theta^* = \arg \min_{\theta} \sum_{T} L_T(f_{\theta}(T))$$

where:

θ is the agent's **meta-policy**,

T represents different tasks,

L_T is the **loss function** for each task.

The goal is to **find an optimal θ** that generalizes well across multiple MARL settings.

Techniques for Meta-Learning in MARL

Several techniques are used to apply meta-learning in MARL, including:

1. Model-Agnostic Meta-Learning (MAML)

MAML trains an agent to find an **initial policy** that is **easily fine-tuned** for new tasks.

Instead of optimizing for **the best performance on one task**, MAML optimizes for **fast adaptation to many tasks**.

MAML Update Rule

$$\theta' = \theta - \alpha \nabla_{\theta} L_T(\theta)$$

where:

θ\theta is the **meta-policy**,

α\alpha is the **learning rate**,

$L_T(\theta)$L_T(\theta) is the **loss function** for a given task TT.

MAML helps agents in MARL environments **adapt quickly** when faced with new cooperative or competitive tasks.

2. Meta Reinforcement Learning via Contextual Embeddings

Instead of training a separate policy for every environment, the agent learns a **context embedding** that helps it adapt dynamically.

The agent **observes the environment** and encodes its dynamics into a **latent representation**.

The **policy is conditioned on this latent variable**, allowing fast adaptation.

This method is effective for MARL tasks **where environments change frequently**, such as:

Autonomous traffic systems with varying road conditions

Multi-robot assembly lines where tasks change dynamically

3. Meta-Q Learning for Multi-Agent Systems

Traditional Q-learning struggles in large-scale MARL settings due to the **curse of dimensionality**.

Meta-Q learning improves this by:

Pre-training agents on multiple tasks, so they learn a **generalizable Q-function**.

Using memory-based architectures to adapt Q-values based on past interactions.

Example: In **multi-agent stock trading**, agents can:

Learn trading patterns from multiple market conditions.

Quickly adapt to new market trends instead of retraining from scratch.

Real-World Applications of Meta-Learning in MARL

1. Autonomous Drones in Disaster Response

Drones deployed in disaster areas **must adapt to new environments quickly**.

Meta-learning allows them to **reuse knowledge from past missions**, improving efficiency in **unfamiliar terrains**.

2. Smart Traffic Systems

A traffic light agent trained in one city should be able to **adapt to new traffic conditions** in another city **without full retraining**.

Meta-learning enables transfer of **traffic control policies** across locations.

3. Multi-Agent Coordination in Video Games

AI teammates in **real-time strategy games** must quickly adapt to **different player behaviors**.

Meta-learning allows AI to **adjust its strategy on the fly** without needing to train from scratch for each new opponent.

Implementing Meta-Learning in MARL (Python Example)

Let's implement **a basic meta-learning agent** that can adapt quickly to **new cooperative tasks** in a **multi-agent grid environment**.

Step 1: Install Dependencies

```
pip install tensorflow numpy gym
```

Step 2: Define the Meta-Learning Agent

```python
import numpy as np
import tensorflow as tf
from tensorflow import keras

class MetaLearningAgent:
    def __init__(self, state_size, action_size):
        self.model = keras.Sequential([
```

```python
            keras.layers.Dense(64,
activation='relu', input_shape=(state_size,)),
            keras.layers.Dense(64,
activation='relu'),
            keras.layers.Dense(action_size,
activation='softmax')
        ])

self.model.compile(optimizer=keras.optimizers.Adam(
learning_rate=0.001),
loss='categorical_crossentropy')

    def adapt(self, state, reward):
        """Quick adaptation based on new
environment experience"""
        with tf.GradientTape() as tape:
            predicted_action = self.model(state)
            loss = -tf.reduce_mean(predicted_action
* reward)
        grads = tape.gradient(loss,
self.model.trainable_variables)

self.model.optimizer.apply_gradients(zip(grads,
self.model.trainable_variables))

# Initialize agents
agent1 = MetaLearningAgent(state_size=4,
action_size=2)
agent2 = MetaLearningAgent(state_size=4,
action_size=2)
```

Step 3: Quick Adaptation Across Tasks

```python
for task in range(5):  # Simulating different MARL
environments
    state = np.random.rand(4)  # Random state
    reward = np.random.rand()  # Simulated reward
    agent1.adapt(state, reward)
    agent2.adapt(state, reward)
```

This method allows agents to **rapidly adapt to new environments**, improving scalability.

Meta-learning provides **a breakthrough approach for scaling MARL**, enabling agents to:

Generalize across environments

Reduce training time significantly

Adapt quickly to new multi-agent interactions

With applications in **robotics, traffic systems, financial AI, and video games**, meta-learning is a key tool for making MARL **scalable and practical for real-world deployment**.

8. Exploration Strategies in Multi-Agent Reinforcement Learning

In **Multi-Agent Reinforcement Learning (MARL)**, agents must explore their environment to learn optimal strategies. Unlike single-agent settings, where an agent only interacts with a fixed environment, MARL introduces additional complexity because multiple agents **learn and adapt simultaneously**. This means that an agent's exploration can **disrupt or be influenced by the actions of other agents**, making the learning process unstable if not handled properly.

Exploration is essential because **blindly exploiting known strategies** may lead to suboptimal policies, while **random exploration can be inefficient**. The challenge is to design exploration strategies that allow agents to **discover better actions while minimizing unnecessary risk and coordination failures**.

This chapter will explore:

How intrinsic motivation and curiosity-driven learning improve exploration

Multi-agent exploration techniques to encourage effective learning

How to balance risk and reward in exploration for stable policy development

---

Intrinsic Motivation and Curiosity-Driven Learning

In reinforcement learning, agents explore their environment to maximize long-term rewards. However, exploration is often **short-sighted** when driven solely by external rewards, leading to **inefficient learning**—especially in complex, sparse-reward environments. This problem becomes even more pronounced in **multi-agent reinforcement learning (MARL)**, where multiple agents interact and adapt simultaneously.

One of the most effective ways to enhance exploration in MARL is by incorporating **intrinsic motivation and curiosity-driven learning**. Instead of waiting for external rewards, agents develop their own **internal drive** to explore unfamiliar states, leading to **more efficient learning, faster adaptation, and better generalization**.

Why Traditional Exploration Methods Struggle in MARL

In standard reinforcement learning, agents explore their environment using methods like **epsilon-greedy** (random action selection with a probability ϵ\epsilon) or **Boltzmann exploration** (sampling actions based on learned values). While effective in single-agent settings, these techniques face several challenges in MARL:

1. Non-Stationarity in Multi-Agent Learning

Since multiple agents are learning at the same time, the environment **keeps changing dynamically**. If an agent finds a good strategy, that strategy may **become obsolete** as other agents adapt. This creates an unstable learning process, making traditional exploration inefficient.

2. Sparse Rewards and Inefficient Learning

Many real-world MARL environments provide **delayed or infrequent rewards**. For example, in a **robotic warehouse**, a robot may only receive a reward after successfully delivering a package. If traditional exploration methods rely purely on **random action selection**, it may take thousands of episodes before the agent stumbles upon an optimal strategy.

3. Overlapping Exploration in Multi-Agent Systems

When multiple agents explore independently, they may repeatedly visit the **same states**, leading to redundant learning and wasted effort. Without coordination, exploration becomes **inefficient** as agents fail to distribute their discoveries effectively.

These challenges make it clear that **purely random exploration is insufficient for MARL**. A better approach is to give agents **an internal motivation to explore**—which is where intrinsic motivation and curiosity come into play.

How Intrinsic Motivation Enhances Exploration

Intrinsic motivation is an **internal drive** that pushes an agent to **explore novel and useful states** even when no external reward is available. This is inspired by how humans learn—we often explore not just for rewards, but because **we are curious about the unknown**.

In reinforcement learning, intrinsic motivation is formalized as an **internal reward signal** that encourages agents to seek out new experiences. This allows agents to:

Prioritize learning from novel interactions instead of repeating known behaviors.

Explore efficiently without needing external guidance.

Improve generalization, making them more adaptable to new environments.

Mathematically, the intrinsic reward $r_{\text{intrinsic}}(s)$ can be defined as:

$$r_{\text{intrinsic}}(s) = \beta \cdot \text{novelty}(s)$$

where:

β is a scaling factor to balance intrinsic and extrinsic rewards.

$\text{novelty}(s)$ measures how surprising or uncertain the state s is.

Types of Intrinsic Motivation in MARL

There are several ways to design intrinsic rewards that help multi-agent systems explore more effectively:

1. Novelty-Based Intrinsic Rewards

Agents receive a higher reward for exploring states **they have not visited frequently**. A common technique is using **state visitation counts**, where rare states provide greater intrinsic rewards.

$$\text{novelty}(s) = \frac{1}{\sqrt{\text{visits}(s) + 1}}$$

Example: In **autonomous vehicle coordination**, cars exploring rarely-used road segments receive **higher intrinsic rewards**, encouraging them to **learn new routes**.

2. Prediction-Based Intrinsic Rewards

Agents learn a model of the environment and reward themselves when they **encounter situations that surprise them**. The idea is that **high prediction error = more novelty = more learning opportunity**.

$$\text{novelty}(s) = \| f(s) - \hat{f}(s) \|$$

where $f(s)$ is the true environment transition and $\hat{f}(s)$ is the agent's prediction.

Example: In **multi-agent drone exploration**, if a drone encounters unexpected wind conditions, it receives **higher intrinsic rewards** for improving its flight model.

3. Social Influence-Based Intrinsic Rewards

In MARL, agents influence each other's learning. An agent may be rewarded based on **how much it changes the behavior of others**—encouraging coordination.

$$r_{\text{intrinsic}}(s, a) = \alpha \cdot \| a - \bar{a} \|$$

where $\bar{a}$ is the average action of other agents.

Example: In **cooperative AI teammates in esports**, an AI that introduces **new team strategies** receives **intrinsic rewards** for its influence.

Curiosity-Driven Learning as a Powerful Tool for Discovery

Curiosity-driven learning is a **special case of intrinsic motivation** where agents are rewarded for **learning about their environment** rather than simply acting randomly.

A curiosity-driven agent actively seeks **novel experiences** by:

Maximizing prediction error—encountering situations where its current model is wrong.

Exploring unfamiliar state-action pairs that lead to more learning.

Example: In **robotic swarm coordination**, robots may receive higher curiosity rewards for **finding new movement patterns** that improve energy efficiency.

Curiosity-driven learning allows MARL agents to:

Discover new strategies faster.

Explore more intelligently without random trial and error.

Learn adaptive behaviors that generalize across environments.

Real-World Applications of Intrinsic Motivation in MARL

Autonomous Exploration Drones

Drones searching for survivors after a disaster **prioritize unknown areas** using curiosity-based intrinsic rewards.

This leads to **efficient search strategies** instead of random flying.

Self-Organizing Swarm Robots

In large warehouses, **robotic fleets must explore optimally** to distribute tasks.

Intrinsic motivation helps them **discover efficient movement patterns** without relying on human programming.

AI-Teammates in Multiplayer Strategy Games

AI teammates in games like **Dota 2 and StarCraft II** use curiosity to **discover new tactics** by exploring **unusual battle formations**.

Implementing Curiosity-Driven Exploration in Python

Let's implement a **simple multi-agent curiosity-driven reinforcement learning system**, where agents explore a gridworld **based on novelty detection**.

Step 1: Install Dependencies

```
pip install tensorflow numpy gym
```

Step 2: Define the Intrinsic Reward Function

```python
import numpy as np
import tensorflow as tf
from tensorflow import keras

class CuriosityAgent:
    def __init__(self, state_size, action_size):
        self.model = keras.Sequential([
            keras.layers.Dense(64,
activation='relu', input_shape=(state_size,)),
            keras.layers.Dense(64,
activation='relu'),
            keras.layers.Dense(action_size,
activation='softmax')
        ])

self.model.compile(optimizer=keras.optimizers.Adam(
learning_rate=0.001),
loss='categorical_crossentropy')
        self.visited_states = {}

    def intrinsic_reward(self, state):
        """Encourages visiting novel states"""
        state_key = tuple(state)
        self.visited_states[state_key] =
self.visited_states.get(state_key, 0) + 1
        return 1 /
np.sqrt(self.visited_states[state_key])

    def train(self, state, reward):
        """Adjust policy using intrinsic rewards"""
        total_reward = reward +
self.intrinsic_reward(state)
        with tf.GradientTape() as tape:
            predicted_action = self.model(state)
            loss = -tf.reduce_mean(predicted_action
* total_reward)
        grads = tape.gradient(loss,
self.model.trainable_variables)
```

```
self.model.optimizer.apply_gradients(zip(grads,
self.model.trainable_variables))
```

This method allows agents to **learn dynamically**, prioritizing exploration in **rarely visited states**.

Intrinsic motivation and curiosity-driven learning **transform MARL by making exploration more efficient, adaptive, and scalable**. These techniques are critical for **real-world AI systems** that must learn in complex, unpredictable environments.

Multi-Agent Exploration Techniques in Reinforcement Learning

In multi-agent reinforcement learning (MARL), agents must explore their environment to discover **optimal strategies**. However, exploration in MARL is significantly more complex than in single-agent reinforcement learning. Since multiple agents are **learning and adapting simultaneously**, their actions influence each other, leading to **unstable learning dynamics** if exploration is not handled correctly.

Poor exploration strategies in MARL can lead to **inefficient learning, redundant searches, coordination failures, and unstable policies**. To address these issues, MARL uses **structured exploration techniques** that enable agents to discover useful policies **while reducing unnecessary risk and inefficiencies**.

Why Exploration is Challenging in Multi-Agent Settings

1. Non-Stationarity Due to Simultaneous Learning

In single-agent reinforcement learning, the environment remains relatively stable—the agent learns from past experiences and updates its policy accordingly.

However, in MARL, every agent is learning at the same time. This means that **the environment itself keeps changing**, making it difficult for agents to

125

develop stable policies. A strategy that worked in one episode may no longer work in the next because **other agents have adapted**.

For example, in **multi-agent stock trading**, one AI may exploit a market inefficiency, but if other agents also discover and exploit it, **the inefficiency disappears**, forcing all agents to continuously relearn strategies.

2. Overlapping Exploration Leads to Inefficiencies

When multiple agents **explore independently**, they may frequently visit **the same states**, leading to redundant learning.

For example, in a **robotic warehouse**, if all robots explore the same aisles repeatedly, they **waste time learning about already known areas** instead of covering unexplored sections.

3. Balancing Competition and Cooperation

In competitive environments, agents **need to explore their opponent's weaknesses**, but too much exploration can lead to **excessive risk-taking**. In cooperative environments, agents need to **explore strategies that benefit the team** while avoiding **selfish exploration** that disrupts coordination.

For example, in **multi-agent traffic control**, if one intersection optimizes its traffic lights without considering nearby intersections, it may reduce local congestion but create gridlock in other areas.

Given these challenges, MARL requires specialized **exploration techniques** to balance **learning efficiency, coordination, and stability**.

Key Multi-Agent Exploration Techniques

1. Shared Experience Replay for Coordinated Learning

One way to improve exploration efficiency in MARL is through **shared experience replay**, where agents share **important experiences** with their teammates.

In traditional reinforcement learning, an agent stores its past experiences in a replay buffer and **reuses them for training**. In MARL, this idea is extended so that **agents can sample experiences from each other**, enabling them to:

Learn from **states visited by other agents**, reducing redundant exploration.

Improve sample efficiency by **leveraging shared knowledge**.

Speed up convergence by allowing agents to **learn collectively instead of individually**.

Implementation Example

```
import random

class SharedExperienceReplay:
    def __init__(self, capacity=10000):
        self.memory = []
        self.capacity = capacity

    def add(self, experience):
        if len(self.memory) >= self.capacity:
            self.memory.pop(0)
        self.memory.append(experience)

    def sample(self, batch_size):
        return random.sample(self.memory,
min(len(self.memory), batch_size))

# Shared buffer for all agents
shared_buffer = SharedExperienceReplay()

# Each agent adds experiences to the buffer
agent_experience = (state, action, reward,
next_state)
shared_buffer.add(agent_experience)

# Any agent can sample from the buffer
batch = shared_buffer.sample(batch_size=32)
```

By sharing experiences, agents **speed up exploration** and avoid learning inefficiencies.

2. Social Influence Exploration: Learning from Other Agents' Actions

Instead of randomly exploring, agents can use **social influence-based exploration**, where they **observe and imitate** successful agents.

This is particularly useful in MARL environments where agents can benefit from following **leaders** or **identifying which agents contribute the most to success**.

In a **multi-agent battlefield simulation**, for example:

Agents that observe successful teammates **adjust their exploration based on high-performing agents**.

Agents that detect **key decision-makers** may follow their strategies instead of exploring independently.

Mathematically, an agent's reward is modified to include an **influence reward**:

$$r_i = r_{\text{environment}} + \alpha \cdot \text{influence}(a_i, a_j)$$

where:

r_i is the total reward for agent i.

$r_{\text{environment}}$ is the normal environment reward.

α is a scaling factor.

$\text{influence}(a_i, a_j)$ measures how much agent j's action a_j affects agent i's policy.

This allows agents to **discover cooperative strategies faster** while still allowing individual learning.

3. Hierarchical Exploration for Task Division

Instead of each agent **exploring blindly**, a structured approach is to use **hierarchical reinforcement learning**, where:

High-level agents decide broad exploration strategies.

Low-level agents execute exploration based on high-level guidance.

This is useful in large-scale **multi-agent robotic systems**, where:

A **centralized planner** assigns different exploration zones to robots.

Each robot **independently explores** its assigned region but communicates back with the planner.

For example, in **search-and-rescue missions**, a fleet of drones can be assigned:

High-level instructions: "Drones 1-3 explore the north zone, Drones 4-6 explore the south zone."

Low-level execution: Each drone **optimizes its flight path** within its assigned area.

By structuring exploration hierarchically, MARL systems **cover more ground efficiently** without redundant learning.

4. Intrinsic Motivation for Novelty-Driven Exploration

Instead of relying only on external rewards, agents can be **intrinsically motivated** to explore **novel and uncertain states**.

This is particularly useful in **sparse reward environments**, where agents may not receive frequent external feedback.

For example, in **multi-agent self-driving cars**, agents can:

Prioritize exploring underutilized routes by assigning higher rewards to **rarely visited roads**.

Learn to adapt to unpredictable traffic conditions by maximizing **novel experiences**.

Implementation Example

```
import numpy as np

class IntrinsicReward:
    def __init__(self):
        self.visited_states = {}

    def novelty_bonus(self, state):
        """Assigns higher rewards to rarely visited
states"""
```

```
        state_key = tuple(state)
        self.visited_states[state_key] =
self.visited_states.get(state_key, 0) + 1
        return 1 /
np.sqrt(self.visited_states[state_key])

# Example use case
intrinsic_reward_module = IntrinsicReward()
state = (2, 3)  # Some state representation
intrinsic_reward =
intrinsic_reward_module.novelty_bonus(state)
```

This allows MARL agents to **explore efficiently while avoiding unnecessary random movements**.

Real-World Applications of Multi-Agent Exploration

Autonomous Traffic Management

Self-driving cars must **coordinate lane-switching strategies** while exploring safe and efficient driving patterns.

Shared experience replay ensures that **all vehicles learn from each other** to reduce congestion.

AI in Multiplayer Esports

AI teammates in games like **Dota 2 and StarCraft II** must balance **exploration and cooperation**.

Social influence-based exploration enables AI players to learn from **successful teammates** while maintaining diversity in strategies.

Industrial Robotics and Warehousing

In automated warehouses, robots must **efficiently explore storage layouts**.

Hierarchical exploration ensures that robots **cover all aisles optimally** without overlap.

Exploration in MARL is **more challenging** than in single-agent settings due to **non-stationarity, redundant exploration, and coordination issues**. By using **shared experience replay, social influence, hierarchical exploration, and intrinsic motivation**, agents can:

Learn more efficiently by leveraging shared knowledge.

Avoid redundant exploration, improving scalability.

Balance competition and cooperation, leading to **smarter multi-agent coordination**.

These exploration strategies are critical for **autonomous vehicles, robotic fleets, AI-driven trading, and adaptive gaming AI**—enabling MARL to scale efficiently in complex real-world environments.

Balancing Risk and Reward in Exploration for MARL

In **Multi-Agent Reinforcement Learning (MARL)**, exploration is essential for discovering **optimal strategies**. However, exploration is not without consequences. Some actions may lead to **high rewards**, while others may result in **catastrophic failures**. This creates a fundamental trade-off:

Exploring risky actions can uncover **new, more rewarding strategies** but may lead to **costly mistakes**.

Playing it safe minimizes failures but **limits learning opportunities**.

Balancing **risk and reward** is even more challenging in MARL because multiple agents are **learning simultaneously**. One agent's decision to take a risk can **affect the entire group**, making it crucial to design exploration strategies that **optimize collective learning while minimizing unnecessary failures**.

Why Balancing Risk and Reward is Critical in MARL

1. The Cost of Exploration in Multi-Agent Systems

In single-agent reinforcement learning, an agent's mistakes **only affect itself**. However, in MARL, one agent's poor decision **can disrupt the learning process for others**.

For example, in **autonomous drone swarms**, one drone taking a high-risk path through a **stormy area** might:

Crash and stop contributing to the mission.

Cause other drones to react suboptimally, leading to **inefficient coordination**.

Balancing **risk and reward** ensures that exploration contributes **positively to collective learning** instead of introducing unnecessary instability.

2. The Challenge of Delayed Rewards

Many MARL environments involve **delayed rewards**, meaning the consequences of an action **may not be immediately visible**.

For instance, in **multi-agent financial trading**, an algorithm may take a **high-risk investment** that appears **profitable in the short term** but leads to **long-term losses** due to market instability.

Without careful exploration strategies, MARL agents may:

Overestimate short-term gains, leading to reckless behavior.

Underestimate the long-term value of safer exploration, leading to **stagnation**.

3. Non-Stationary Multi-Agent Environments

Since agents learn simultaneously, the **environment constantly shifts**. This means that **risky actions that were beneficial yesterday** may no longer be useful today.

For example, in **self-driving fleets**, a car may explore **an aggressive overtaking maneuver** that works in light traffic. However, as other cars **adapt to this strategy**, it may **increase the risk of collisions**.

A well-balanced exploration strategy must account for **changing conditions** and adjust **risk tolerance dynamically**.

Techniques for Balancing Risk and Reward in Exploration

1. Risk-Aware Exploration with Uncertainty Estimation

One way to manage risk is to estimate **how uncertain an agent is about an action's outcome**. If an action has a **high level of uncertainty**, it can be explored **gradually** instead of **immediately committing to it**.

Mathematically, uncertainty can be estimated using **Bayesian approaches** or **ensemble learning**, where multiple neural networks predict an action's outcome, and **the variance of their predictions** determines uncertainty:

$$\text{Uncertainty}(a) = \text{Var}\left[Q_{\theta_1}(s, a), Q_{\theta_2}(s, a), ..., Q_{\theta_n}(s, a) \right]$$

where $Q_{\theta_i}(s, a)$ is the Q-value predicted by different models.

Actions with **high uncertainty** can be explored **cautiously** by:

Reducing the probability of selecting them in early training.

Gradually increasing exposure as more data becomes available.

Implementation Example

```
import numpy as np

class RiskAwareExploration:
    def __init__(self, action_size):
        self.q_ensemble =
[np.random.rand(action_size) for _ in range(5)]  #
Simulated ensemble of Q-values

    def estimate_uncertainty(self, action):
        """Computes variance across multiple Q-
value predictions to estimate uncertainty"""
        q_values = np.array([q[action] for q in
self.q_ensemble])
        return np.var(q_values)

    def select_action(self, exploration_rate):
        """Chooses an action with reduced
probability for high-uncertainty actions"""
        action_uncertainties =
[self.estimate_uncertainty(a) for a in
range(len(self.q_ensemble[0]))]
```

```
        safe_actions = np.exp(-
np.array(action_uncertainties))  # Convert to
probabilities (lower uncertainty -> higher prob)
        safe_actions /= np.sum(safe_actions)
        return
np.random.choice(range(len(safe_actions)),
p=safe_actions)

# Example usage
explorer = RiskAwareExploration(action_size=4)
chosen_action =
explorer.select_action(exploration_rate=0.2)
print(f"Selected action: {chosen_action}")
```

This approach ensures that **high-risk actions are gradually explored** while prioritizing safer choices.

2. Dynamic Risk Adjustment with Reward Scaling

In dynamic environments, agents should **adjust their risk-taking behavior** based on performance. If **recent exploratory actions have been successful**, the agent can afford to **take more risks**. If exploration has led to **poor outcomes**, the agent should **become more conservative**.

A common method is **reward scaling**, where the agent's exploration probability is modified based on recent performance:

$$\epsilon = \epsilon_{\text{min}} + (\epsilon_{\text{max}} - \epsilon_{\text{min}}) \times e^{-k \cdot R_{\text{recent}}}$$

where:

ϵ_{min} and ϵ_{max} set the range of exploration probabilities.

R_{recent} is the **recent average reward**.

k controls how fast risk-taking decays.

If recent rewards are **high**, exploration decreases **slowly** (allowing risk-taking). If rewards are **low**, exploration **drops sharply** (encouraging caution).

134

Example Application: Multi-Agent Traffic Control

In **adaptive traffic signal control**, exploration should be **riskier when traffic is light** (to test new signal timings) and **more conservative during rush hour** (to avoid congestion).

Using dynamic risk adjustment, the traffic control system can:

Explore alternate routes when traffic is low.

Prioritize stability during high-demand periods.

3. Safe Exploration with Risk-Constrained Optimization

Another approach is **constraining exploration within predefined safety limits**. Agents can **explore freely**, but only **within safe thresholds** defined by a risk function:

$$\max_{\pi} E_{\pi}[R] \quad \text{subject to} \quad E_{\pi}[\text{Risk}] \leq \delta$$

where:

R is the expected reward.

Risk is a predefined measure of safety (e.g., probability of failure).

δ is a risk threshold.

This ensures that exploration does not exceed **acceptable safety limits**, making it suitable for **autonomous systems operating in high-stakes environments**.

Example: Industrial Robotics

In **automated warehouses**, robotic arms must **test new grasping techniques** while ensuring **objects are not damaged**.

A risk-constrained policy prevents **excessively forceful grasps** while still allowing **new techniques to be explored**.

Real-World Applications of Risk-Aware Exploration

1. Self-Driving Fleets

Cars must explore **new overtaking strategies** while **ensuring safe distances**.

Risk-aware exploration prevents reckless behavior in **high-speed conditions**.

2. AI in Financial Trading

Trading bots must test **new market strategies** while avoiding **excessive exposure** to volatile assets.

Dynamic risk adjustment **reduces aggressive trading after heavy losses**.

3. AI-Powered Healthcare Optimization

AI-driven **treatment recommendation systems** must explore **alternative therapies** while ensuring **patient safety**.

Constrained exploration prevents **high-risk recommendations** in critical care.

Balancing **risk and reward** in MARL exploration is essential for **efficient learning, safe adaptation, and long-term success**. Using techniques like **uncertainty estimation, dynamic risk scaling, and risk-constrained optimization**, agents can explore intelligently **without unnecessary failures**.

These methods are crucial for **self-driving vehicles, financial AI, robotics, and large-scale decision-making systems**, where safe and efficient exploration defines success.

9. Transfer Learning and Generalization in MARL

In traditional reinforcement learning, agents must learn optimal behaviors from scratch for every new environment. This process is slow, data-intensive, and computationally expensive. In **Multi-Agent Reinforcement Learning (MARL)**, the challenge is even greater—agents must learn **not only how to act individually but also how to interact with other agents**, which adds an additional layer of complexity.

What if agents could transfer knowledge across environments? Instead of learning everything from the beginning, agents could use prior experience to **adapt quickly to new tasks, new environments, and even new teammates**. This is the core idea behind **transfer learning and generalization in MARL**.

Domain Adaptation in Multi-Agent Reinforcement Learning

In **Multi-Agent Reinforcement Learning (MARL)**, agents are trained to interact with an environment and optimize their collective behaviors. However, training is often limited to **a specific environment**, and when agents are deployed in **a different but related environment**, their learned policies may fail. This is because small changes in environmental dynamics—such as different terrain for robots, varied traffic conditions for self-driving fleets, or different opponent strategies in multi-agent games—can **disrupt previously learned behaviors**.

Domain adaptation in MARL addresses this challenge by enabling agents to **transfer their learned knowledge from one environment (the source domain) to another environment (the target domain) with minimal additional training**. Instead of re-learning everything from scratch, agents learn to **generalize and adapt**, making them more efficient and flexible in real-world applications.

Why Domain Adaptation is Essential in MARL

The Problem: Transferability of MARL Policies Across Environments

A policy trained in one environment is optimized for the **specific characteristics of that environment**. But what happens when we introduce a slightly different environment?

Consider an example in **multi-agent warehouse robotics**:

A fleet of robots trained to **move pallets in a structured warehouse layout** might struggle if deployed in a **new warehouse with different aisle widths and shelf placements**.

If the new warehouse has **more unpredictable human movement**, previously learned collision avoidance strategies may become **suboptimal or unsafe**.

Without domain adaptation, the agents must **start learning from scratch**, which is computationally expensive and time-consuming.

The Importance of Adaptation

Domain adaptation allows MARL agents to:

Reduce training time when shifting to new environments.

Leverage prior knowledge to adapt faster instead of learning from zero.

Improve real-world deployment of MARL agents across different operational conditions.

If robots, self-driving cars, or AI teammates in online games could **adapt efficiently** across different domains, we could **scale MARL systems more effectively in real-world applications**.

Challenges of Adapting MARL Agents Across Domains

1. Domain Shift in Environmental Dynamics

A domain shift occurs when key environmental variables **change slightly or significantly**. Even small differences can lead to **significant performance degradation**.

For example, in **multi-agent autonomous drone swarms**, a change in:

Wind conditions can affect flight stability.

Air density at different altitudes can alter battery consumption.

GPS reliability in urban vs. rural areas can impact navigation accuracy.

A drone policy trained in **one set of conditions** may struggle in **another set of conditions** if it is not adapted properly.

2. Non-Stationarity Due to Multi-Agent Interactions

Since multiple agents interact in MARL, **adapting one agent's policy** can disrupt the learning process for others. If an agent **suddenly behaves differently** in a new domain, its teammates or competitors **must also adapt**, making stable learning more difficult.

3. Partial Observability and Communication Differences

In cooperative MARL tasks, agents may rely on **shared observations and communication protocols**. However, domain adaptation might introduce **different levels of communication availability** or **different sensor modalities**, making the transfer of knowledge harder.

For example, in **multi-agent robotic search-and-rescue**, agents trained in **simulated environments with perfect sensor data** might struggle in **real-world disaster zones with sensor noise and communication delays**.

Techniques for Domain Adaptation in MARL

1. Domain Randomization for Robust Learning

Instead of training MARL agents in a **single fixed environment**, domain randomization exposes them to **a variety of slightly different environments** during training. This forces agents to learn **robust policies** that generalize better to new domains.

Example: Training Self-Driving Fleets with Varying Traffic Patterns

A fleet of self-driving cars can be trained using **randomized traffic conditions, weather, and road layouts** instead of a fixed dataset. When deployed in a real city, the learned policy is **more adaptable to unseen conditions**.

Mathematically, the agent's objective is:

$$\pi* = \arg\max_{\pi} \mathbb{E}_{P(s'|s,a)} [R(s, a)]$$

where $P(s'|s,a)$ is sampled from a **distribution of possible domains** rather than a single environment.

Python Example: Domain Randomization for MARL Training

```python
import numpy as np

class RandomizedEnvironment:
    def __init__(self):
        self.wind_conditions = np.random.uniform(0,
1)   # Vary wind strength
        self.traffic_density = np.random.uniform(0,
1)   # Vary traffic conditions

    def get_state(self):
        return np.array([self.wind_conditions,
self.traffic_density])

# Training loop with randomized environments
for episode in range(100):
    env = RandomizedEnvironment()   # Create a new
randomized environment
    state = env.get_state()
    print(f"Training in environment with
wind={state[0]:.2f}, traffic={state[1]:.2f}")
```

This ensures that MARL agents are **exposed to diverse scenarios**, making them more robust during deployment.

2. Feature Alignment Across Domains

If the **state representation** of two domains is different, MARL agents struggle to transfer knowledge. **Feature alignment** maps source domain states to target domain states to create a **common representation space**.

Example: Translating Simulation Data to Real-World Robotics

A robotic system trained in **simulated environments** may not directly transfer to real-world deployment due to differences in **sensor data distribution**.

Solution: Use **adversarial domain adaptation**, where a neural network learns to align feature distributions between the source and target domains.

$$\min_{\theta} \max_{D} \sum_{x \in S, T} D(f_{\theta}(x)) - \sum_{x \in T} D(f_{\theta}(x))$$

where D is a domain discriminator trying to distinguish between **source domain (S) states** and **target domain (T) states**. The agent learns a feature representation $f_{\theta}(x)$ that makes them indistinguishable.

3. Reward Shaping for Adaptation

Instead of forcing agents to **relearn behaviors**, reward shaping guides their exploration in the new domain. By modifying the reward function based on **how different the new domain is**, agents learn more efficiently.

Example: Adapting Multi-Agent Soccer AI to New Tactics

An AI trained in **European football strategies** might struggle in **South American football, where player movement is different**.

Solution: Use a shaped reward function to **penalize deviations from the new strategy** while still allowing the agent to explore.

$$R'(s, a) = R(s, a) - \lambda \cdot ||\pi_{\text{new}}(s) - \pi_{\text{old}}(s)||$$

where λ controls how much the agent **penalizes deviation from learned behaviors** while adapting.

Real-World Applications of Domain Adaptation in MARL

1. Autonomous Vehicles Across Cities

Self-driving cars trained in one city (e.g., **Los Angeles**) should adapt to another city (e.g., **Tokyo**) without **retraining from scratch**.

Domain adaptation helps adjust to **new road signs, driving behavior, and traffic laws**.

2. Adaptive AI in Competitive Multiplayer Games

AI teammates trained for **one esports team strategy** must adapt to **different team compositions** in competitive play.

3. Warehouse Robotics with Changing Layouts

Robots trained in a **structured warehouse** must adapt when deployed in **unstructured environments** with **dynamic shelving positions**.

Domain adaptation is crucial for making MARL agents **scalable, efficient, and generalizable** across different environments. Techniques such as **domain randomization, feature alignment, and reward shaping** enable agents to **transfer knowledge across tasks and environments**, reducing training time and improving real-world performance.

With continued advancements, MARL agents will be able to **adapt seamlessly to new environments** in **robotics, autonomous driving, financial markets, and large-scale AI systems**—making AI-powered multi-agent collaboration more practical than ever.

Zero-Shot and Few-Shot Learning for Agents

Traditional reinforcement learning relies on **repeated interactions** with the environment to learn optimal policies. However, in real-world multi-agent systems, this approach is **impractical** when agents need to adapt to new tasks or environments **quickly**.

For example, an autonomous **fleet of delivery drones** trained in one city should be able to operate in a new city **without weeks of retraining**. Similarly, a robotic **warehouse team** should adapt when a new product type is introduced **without starting from scratch**.

This is where **zero-shot and few-shot learning** become essential. These methods enable agents to:

Zero-shot learning (ZSL): Adapt to new tasks or environments **without any additional training**.

Few-shot learning (FSL): Adapt using **only a small number of new training examples**.

These approaches allow MARL agents to **generalize** from prior experiences, significantly reducing training time and improving efficiency in dynamic environments.

Why Zero-Shot and Few-Shot Learning Are Crucial in MARL

1. Eliminating the Need for Retraining

In traditional MARL, every new task requires **retraining from scratch**, which is time-consuming and computationally expensive. With ZSL and FSL, agents can **transfer prior knowledge** to new situations, making learning more efficient.

2. Adapting to Dynamic Multi-Agent Environments

Multi-agent environments are **constantly changing**. An agent may encounter **new teammates, opponents, or task variations** that were not present during training. Without the ability to generalize, agents will **struggle to adapt**.

For example, in **real-time strategy (RTS) games** like StarCraft II:

AI teammates must **quickly adjust** to new player strategies.

Learning from **just a few examples** of a new strategy allows AI to adapt **without starting from zero**.

3. Reducing Sample Inefficiency in MARL

MARL environments often have **sparse rewards**, meaning useful feedback is rare. **Few-shot learning** enables agents to extract **maximum knowledge from minimal interactions**, improving efficiency in data-scarce environments.

For instance, in **autonomous vehicle coordination**, testing in real traffic is expensive. A few-shot learning approach allows vehicles to:

Adapt to **new city layouts** after a few test drives.

Transfer learned policies **from highway driving to urban traffic** without full retraining.

Techniques for Zero-Shot and Few-Shot Learning in MARL

1. Meta-Learning for Fast Adaptation

Meta-learning, often called **"learning to learn,"** enables agents to extract general knowledge from multiple MARL tasks, making them adaptable to new environments **with minimal data**.

How Meta-Learning Works

Instead of training an agent for a **single** environment, it is trained across **multiple** environments. The goal is to learn a policy that is **highly adaptable** rather than overfitting to one specific task.

During training, the agent's objective is to **minimize loss across multiple tasks**, optimizing for adaptability:

$$\theta^* = \arg \min_{\theta} \sum_{T} L_T(f_{\theta}(T))$$

where:

θ is the **meta-learned policy**.

T represents **different tasks or environments**.

L_T is the loss function for each task.

Once trained, the agent can **quickly fine-tune** itself for new tasks **with minimal data**.

Example: Few-Shot Learning for Multi-Agent Drone Swarms

A **fleet of search-and-rescue drones** trained in a **mountainous environment** should be able to adapt to a **forest environment** using **just a few flights**.

Meta-learning enables them to:

Transfer learned **obstacle avoidance strategies** to new terrains.

Adjust their **communication protocols** with minimal retraining.

2. Policy Distillation for Zero-Shot Generalization

Policy distillation allows an agent to **learn from multiple trained policies** and generalize to **unseen tasks**.

Instead of learning a new policy for each environment, a single **generalized policy** is distilled from **multiple expert demonstrations**.

$$\pi*(s)=\sum i=1 N w_i \pi_i(s) \pi^*(s) = \sum_{i=1}^{N} w_i \pi_i(s)$$

where:

$\pi i(s)\pi_i(s)$ are **expert policies** trained in different environments.

$w_i w\_i$ are learned **weights** that determine how much to rely on each expert policy.

Example: Self-Driving Cars Adapting to New Cities Without Retraining

A car trained in **New York, Los Angeles, and Paris** can generalize to **Tokyo** without new training data.

The learned policy uses features **common to all cities** (e.g., lane discipline) while **adjusting to local differences** (e.g., driving on the left side of the road).

3. Embedding-Based Few-Shot Learning

Instead of learning raw state-action mappings, agents **encode experiences into embeddings** that capture **abstract relationships** between different tasks.

By representing states as embeddings, an agent can **compare new tasks to previously seen tasks** and **find the most relevant learned behaviors**.

$$f embed(s)=MLP(s)f_{\text{embed}}(s) = \text{MLP}(s)$$

where $f embed(s) f\_{\text{embed}}\}(s)$ maps a state $s s$ into a **latent space** shared across multiple tasks.

Example: Robotics Task Transfer

A robotic arm trained to **assemble furniture** can learn a **new type of chair** by comparing its structure to **previously assembled chairs** using embeddings.

Real-World Applications of Zero-Shot and Few-Shot Learning in MARL

1. Adaptive AI Teammates in Video Games

AI teammates in **multiplayer esports** need to **adapt instantly** when paired with new human players.

Zero-shot learning enables them to **recognize playstyles** and adjust **without needing additional training matches**.

2. Smart Traffic Systems for Different Cities

A traffic control system trained in one city should **function in another** without retraining.

Few-shot learning enables fast adaptation **using only a few hours of local traffic data**.

3. Autonomous Warehouses with Changing Inventory

Robots should adjust to **new warehouse layouts** without full retraining.

Few-shot learning allows them to **learn new item placements from a few observations**.

Implementing Few-Shot Learning for MARL in Python

Let's implement a **meta-learning agent** that adapts to new MARL tasks **using minimal data**.

Step 1: Install Dependencies

```
pip install tensorflow numpy gym
```

Step 2: Define the Few-Shot Learning MARL Agent

```python
import numpy as np
import tensorflow as tf
from tensorflow import keras

class FewShotMARLAgent:
    def __init__(self, state_size, action_size):
        self.model = keras.Sequential([
            keras.layers.Dense(64,
activation='relu', input_shape=(state_size,)),
```

```
            keras.layers.Dense(64,
activation='relu'),
            keras.layers.Dense(action_size,
activation='softmax')
        ])

self.model.compile(optimizer=keras.optimizers.Adam(
learning_rate=0.001),
loss='categorical_crossentropy')

    def adapt(self, new_task_data):
        """Fine-tunes the agent on a new task with
minimal data"""
        self.model.fit(new_task_data['states'],
new_task_data['actions'], epochs=3, verbose=1)

# Train agent on initial MARL tasks
agent = FewShotMARLAgent(state_size=4,
action_size=2)

# Transfer to a new task with few-shot adaptation
new_task_data = {'states': np.random.rand(10, 4),
'actions': np.random.rand(10, 2)}
agent.adapt(new_task_data)
```

This enables the agent to **quickly adapt to new tasks** with minimal data, making it ideal for **real-world MARL applications**.

Zero-shot and few-shot learning are essential for **scaling MARL systems** to real-world applications. Using techniques like **meta-learning, policy distillation, and embedding-based learning**, agents can **adapt to new environments, tasks, and teammates efficiently**—reducing training time and making MARL **more practical in dynamic settings**.

Multi-Agent Meta-Learning Approaches

In multi-agent reinforcement learning (MARL), agents interact with their environment and each other to learn optimal behaviors. However, traditional MARL methods often struggle with **adaptability and scalability** when deployed in **new tasks, environments, or teams**. This is because most training approaches optimize for **specific tasks**, making agents perform well in the training setup but **struggle in unseen scenarios**.

Multi-agent meta-learning addresses this limitation by **training agents to learn efficiently from new experiences** rather than simply memorizing policies. Instead of optimizing for a single task, meta-learning optimizes for **adaptability**, enabling agents to **generalize across different environments and adapt with minimal data**.

Why Meta-Learning is Essential in Multi-Agent Systems

1. Multi-Agent Systems Face Constantly Changing Environments

Unlike single-agent RL, where an agent interacts with a mostly **static environment**, MARL introduces **non-stationarity**—every agent's learning process **affects the environment for others**.

For example, in **multi-agent autonomous traffic control**:

If one traffic light optimizes for faster flow, it **changes traffic patterns**, requiring other intersections to **adjust their timing strategies dynamically**.

A policy trained in one city **may fail in another city** with different traffic laws.

2. Learning From Scratch is Computationally Expensive

Training multi-agent systems from scratch in every new environment **requires significant time and resources**. Meta-learning enables agents to **reuse prior knowledge**, drastically **reducing training time** in new environments.

Consider a **fleet of autonomous drones** trained for **urban delivery routes**:

If the same drones are deployed in a **suburban area**, they should **adapt using minimal experience** instead of re-learning everything.

3. Adapting to New Teammates or Opponents

In competitive environments like **multi-agent esports AI**, teams change frequently.

A meta-learning agent trained on **various team compositions** can quickly adjust to **new teammates** or **opponents with different playstyles**.

Instead of memorizing fixed strategies, meta-learning allows agents to **learn how to learn**, enabling generalization to **unseen scenarios**.

Key Techniques for Multi-Agent Meta-Learning

1. Model-Agnostic Meta-Learning (MAML) for Fast Adaptation

MAML is a gradient-based meta-learning method that **optimizes agents to adapt quickly to new tasks**. Instead of training a fixed policy, MAML finds an **initial policy** that can be **fine-tuned rapidly** with just a few gradient updates.

How MAML Works in MARL

During training:

The meta-policy θ\theta is **trained on multiple MARL environments**.

The agent performs a few gradient updates **in each new task**.

The final update optimizes θ\theta so that adaptation happens **efficiently** when exposed to a new task.

The objective function is:

$$\theta^* = \arg\min_{\theta} \theta \sum_{T} L_T(f\theta(T)) \backslash theta^\wedge* = \backslash arg \backslash min\_\{\backslash theta\} \backslash sum\_\{T\} L\_T(f\_\{\backslash theta\}(T))$$

where:

θ\theta is the **meta-policy** optimized for fast adaptation.

TT represents different MARL tasks.

LTL_T is the loss function for task TT.

Example: Meta-Learning for Multi-Agent Search-and-Rescue Robots

Robots trained in **earthquake-damaged buildings** should be able to **adapt to forest rescue missions** with minimal retraining.

MAML enables them to **learn general navigation principles** that can be **fine-tuned for new terrain conditions**.

Python Example: MAML for MARL Agents

```python
import numpy as np
import tensorflow as tf
from tensorflow import keras

class MAMLMARLAgent:
    def __init__(self, state_size, action_size):
        self.model = keras.Sequential([
            keras.layers.Dense(64,
activation='relu', input_shape=(state_size,)),
            keras.layers.Dense(64,
activation='relu'),
            keras.layers.Dense(action_size,
activation='softmax')
        ])

self.model.compile(optimizer=keras.optimizers.Adam(
learning_rate=0.001),
loss='categorical_crossentropy')

    def adapt(self, task_data):
        """Performs a few-shot adaptation on new
MARL tasks"""
        self.model.fit(task_data['states'],
task_data['actions'], epochs=3, verbose=1)

# Initialize an agent with meta-learning capability
meta_agent = MAMLMARLAgent(state_size=4,
action_size=2)

# Adapt to a new multi-agent task
new_task_data = {'states': np.random.rand(10, 4),
'actions': np.random.rand(10, 2)}
meta_agent.adapt(new_task_data)
```

This allows the agent to **quickly fine-tune itself for new MARL environments** with minimal data.

2. Meta Reinforcement Learning with Contextual Embeddings

Instead of learning raw state-action mappings, meta-learning agents **encode experiences into embeddings** that capture **generalizable features**.

By mapping different MARL tasks into a **latent representation**, agents can compare **new tasks** to previous experiences and quickly adapt.

This allows agents to **transfer knowledge** even when facing **entirely new state-action spaces**.

Example: AI in Multi-Agent Board Games

An AI trained in **chess** should be able to **transfer strategic knowledge** to **Go**, despite different rules.

Contextual embeddings allow it to recognize **game structure similarities** and adapt accordingly.

3. Multi-Agent Meta-Reinforcement Learning (Meta-RL)

Meta-RL enables agents to **infer task structures** from limited interactions instead of requiring explicit instructions.

Agents use **Bayesian inference** to estimate the underlying task distribution, adjusting their policies accordingly.

This technique is useful in **ad-hoc teamwork scenarios**, where agents must **collaborate with unseen teammates**.

Example: Robotics in Dynamic Industrial Environments

A robot trained in **one factory layout** should infer the **task structure of a new factory** based on a few initial interactions.

Meta-RL allows it to recognize common **assembly line structures** and adapt efficiently.

Real-World Applications of Multi-Agent Meta-Learning

1. Autonomous Fleets for Delivery and Transportation

Delivery drones should **adapt to different city layouts** after just a few test flights.

Meta-learning enables them to generalize across **varied urban conditions**.

2. AI-Powered Financial Trading Bots

AI agents trained in one stock market should **adapt to different markets** with minimal data.

Meta-learning allows financial AI to **transfer strategies from one economic condition to another**.

3. AI for Multiplayer Video Games

AI teammates in **esports games** need to **adjust instantly to human player styles**.

Meta-learning ensures that AI players **don't require extensive retraining for every new opponent**.

Multi-agent meta-learning transforms MARL by **shifting the focus from task-specific optimization to rapid adaptability**. Using techniques like **MAML, contextual embeddings, and Meta-RL**, MARL agents become **capable of generalizing across environments and adapting with minimal data**.

These methods enable real-world applications in **robotics, autonomous vehicles, esports AI, and financial trading**, making multi-agent systems more **scalable, efficient, and practical**.

10. Real-World Applications and Case Studies of MARL

Multi-Agent Reinforcement Learning (MARL) has evolved from theoretical research into a practical tool for **solving complex, real-world problems**. Many modern systems require **decentralized decision-making, dynamic adaptation, and large-scale coordination**, making MARL a **powerful approach** for these domains.

From **swarm robotics** optimizing industrial automation to **smart grids** managing energy distribution, MARL enables intelligent agents to **collaborate, compete, and learn** in ways that traditional rule-based systems cannot achieve.

Swarm Robotics and Decentralized Control

Swarm robotics is an advanced area of robotics inspired by **biological swarms**, such as **ants, bees, and fish schools**, where **multiple autonomous agents** work together to achieve collective goals. Unlike traditional robotic systems that rely on **centralized control**, swarm robotics leverages **decentralized decision-making**, where each agent **interacts with local neighbors** to achieve global coordination.

This decentralized control allows robotic swarms to be:

Scalable—The same algorithms can control a handful or thousands of robots.

Resilient—The system remains operational even if some robots fail.

Adaptive—The swarm can self-organize based on environmental conditions.

Swarm robotics is applied in **search-and-rescue, warehouse automation, environmental monitoring, precision agriculture, and military reconnaissance**. This discussion will break down how **multi-agent reinforcement learning (MARL)** enables swarm robotics, key decentralized control techniques, real-world applications, and a practical implementation example.

Why Decentralized Control is Essential in Swarm Robotics

1. The Limitations of Centralized Control

In traditional robotics, a **centralized system** coordinates all robots. While this works for **small-scale systems**, it becomes **computationally expensive and inefficient** as the number of robots increases.

For example, in a **warehouse automation system**, a centralized controller:

Tracks all robots simultaneously.

Calculates optimal paths for each robot.

Updates every robot's movement in real time.

This approach is feasible for **a dozen robots**, but as the fleet scales to **hundreds or thousands**, communication delays and processing bottlenecks **cause failures**.

2. The Benefits of Decentralized Control

Decentralized control allows each robot to **operate autonomously**, making decisions based on **local sensor data and communication with nearby robots**. This provides several advantages:

Fault Tolerance—If one or more robots fail, the rest of the swarm continues operating.

Reduced Communication Overhead—Robots do not need to send all data to a central controller.

Real-Time Adaptability—Each robot responds to environmental changes instantly without waiting for external commands.

For example, in **drone-based search-and-rescue operations**, each drone:

Detects obstacles independently.

Assigns itself to unexplored areas.

Communicates **only with nearby drones** to avoid redundant searches.

This decentralized approach allows drones to **search larger areas efficiently without constant supervision**.

Techniques for Decentralized Swarm Control in MARL

1. Behavior-Based Control

One of the simplest decentralized control strategies is **behavior-based control**, where robots follow predefined **local rules** to achieve global coordination.

For example, in **robotic fish schooling**, each robot follows three simple rules:

Separation—Avoid collisions with nearby robots.

Alignment—Match the movement direction of neighbors.

Cohesion—Stay close to nearby robots.

Mathematically, the velocity v_i of robot i is updated as:

$$v_i = w_s \cdot v_{\text{separation}} + w_a \cdot v_{\text{alignment}} + w_c \cdot v_{\text{cohesion}}$$

where w_s, w_a, w_c are weights for each behavior.

2. Leader-Follower Models

In some swarm robotics applications, a small number of **leader robots** make strategic decisions while **follower robots** adapt their behavior accordingly.

For example, in **multi-robot convoy systems**, a lead robot plans the path, while others:

Adjust speed to maintain **formation stability**.

Detect and respond to **leader slowdowns or obstacles**.

Use **local communication** to share updates with nearby robots.

3. Multi-Agent Reinforcement Learning (MARL) for Swarm Robotics

While behavior-based and leader-follower approaches work well in **structured environments**, they struggle in **dynamic environments** where robots must learn and adapt over time.

MARL enables swarm robots to:

Learn optimal movement patterns from experience.

Adapt dynamically when new obstacles, adversaries, or environmental changes occur.

Optimize swarm efficiency by reinforcing behaviors that lead to successful coordination.

Each robot **learns independently**, but rewards are designed to encourage **cooperative behavior**:

$$R_{\text{global}} = \sum_{i=1}^{N} R_i$$

where R_i is the individual reward of robot i, and R_{global} ensures the swarm **optimizes team performance** rather than individual success.

Real-World Applications of Swarm Robotics

1. Warehouse Automation with Robotic Fleets

Amazon's **Kiva robots** use decentralized control to:

Optimize **package retrieval** and sorting.

Coordinate movement in **high-density storage areas**.

Reduce delivery times by **avoiding congestion**.

2. Agricultural Swarms for Precision Farming

Autonomous robots plant, fertilize, and monitor crops.

Swarm control ensures **robots cover the entire field** efficiently.

Decentralized learning enables **adaptive spraying based on real-time crop health data**.

3. Drone Swarms for Environmental Monitoring

Swarms of drones track **wildlife movements** and **deforestation patterns**.

Decentralized MARL enables them to **coordinate flight paths autonomously**.

Individual drones communicate only when necessary, **reducing bandwidth usage**.

4. Military and Disaster Response

Swarm robots locate **trapped survivors** in collapsed buildings.

Decentralized algorithms **ensure full area coverage** without overlap.

MARL-based coordination enables real-time **route adaptation** in unstable environments.

Implementing Decentralized Swarm Robotics in Python

Let's implement a **basic MARL-based decentralized swarm** where robots navigate an environment while avoiding collisions.

Step 1: Install Dependencies

```
pip install numpy tensorflow keras
```

Step 2: Define the Swarm Robot Agent

```python
import numpy as np
import tensorflow as tf
from tensorflow import keras

class SwarmRobot:
    def __init__(self, state_size, action_size):
        self.model = keras.Sequential([
            keras.layers.Dense(64,
activation='relu', input_shape=(state_size,)),
            keras.layers.Dense(64,
activation='relu'),
            keras.layers.Dense(action_size,
activation='softmax')
        ])

self.model.compile(optimizer=keras.optimizers.Adam(
```

```python
learning_rate=0.001),
loss='categorical_crossentropy')

    def select_action(self, state):
        """Chooses an action based on the robot's
learned policy"""
        action_probabilities =
self.model.predict(np.array([state]))[0]
        return np.argmax(action_probabilities)

    def train(self, state, action, reward,
next_state):
        """Updates the policy using Q-learning"""
        target = reward + 0.9 *
np.max(self.model.predict(np.array([next_state]))[0
])
        target_vector =
self.model.predict(np.array([state]))[0]
        target_vector[action] = target
        self.model.fit(np.array([state]),
np.array([target_vector]), epochs=1, verbose=0)

# Initialize a swarm of 10 robots
robots = [SwarmRobot(state_size=4, action_size=3)
for _ in range(10)]
```

Step 3: Simulating Decentralized Decision-Making

```python
# Simulated environment (random states and rewards)
for episode in range(100):
    for robot in robots:
        state = np.random.rand(4)  # Randomized
sensor input
        action = robot.select_action(state)
        reward = np.random.rand()  # Simulated
feedback
        next_state = np.random.rand(4)
        robot.train(state, action, reward,
next_state)

print("Training complete. Robots can now navigate
the environment using learned behaviors.")
```

This implementation enables robots to **learn cooperative behaviors**, optimizing navigation and obstacle avoidance **without centralized control**.

Swarm robotics and decentralized control are revolutionizing **logistics, agriculture, environmental science, and disaster response**. By integrating **multi-agent reinforcement learning**, robotic swarms **self-organize, learn optimal coordination strategies, and adapt to real-world conditions**.

Decentralized MARL approaches **eliminate bottlenecks of centralized systems**, making them **scalable, resilient, and highly efficient**—an essential step toward the future of autonomous multi-agent systems.

Smart Grid Energy Management Using MARL

A **smart grid** is an intelligent energy system that uses **real-time monitoring, adaptive control, and automation** to optimize the **generation, distribution, and consumption** of electricity. Unlike traditional power grids, which rely on **centralized control**, a smart grid leverages **decentralized decision-making** to improve efficiency, reduce energy waste, and integrate renewable energy sources like **solar and wind power**.

However, managing a smart grid is highly complex due to:

Fluctuating electricity demand throughout the day.

Variable renewable energy production due to changing weather conditions.

Grid stability requirements to prevent power failures.

Market-based electricity pricing that affects energy costs.

Multi-Agent Reinforcement Learning (MARL) provides a scalable and decentralized solution for optimizing energy management by enabling grid operators, energy producers, and consumers to make autonomous, data-driven decisions.

Challenges in Modern Smart Grid Energy Management

1. Balancing Energy Supply and Demand

Electricity demand fluctuates **throughout the day** due to:

Morning and evening peak hours when residential use is high.

Variable industrial energy consumption based on production schedules.

Changing weather conditions affecting heating and cooling systems.

Traditional grids handle this with **backup power plants**, which are expensive and environmentally unsustainable. A smart grid **predicts demand patterns** and **allocates energy dynamically**.

2. Integrating Renewable Energy Sources

Solar and wind power are **unpredictable**—energy production depends on **weather conditions** rather than fixed schedules.

For example:

Solar panels generate excess power during the day but none at night.

Wind turbines fluctuate based on wind speed, sometimes producing too much or too little power.

A smart grid must:

Store excess renewable energy in batteries.

Distribute power dynamically to prevent shortages.

Use demand-side management to incentivize energy consumption when production is high.

3. Decentralized Energy Trading and Pricing

In a smart grid, energy consumers can also be **energy producers** (e.g., homes with solar panels). This introduces **peer-to-peer (P2P) energy trading**, where households sell excess electricity back to the grid or directly to neighbors.

An effective energy management system must:

Determine fair electricity prices dynamically.

Decide when to buy/sell electricity based on market conditions.

Coordinate transactions without centralized control.

4. Grid Stability and Fault Detection

Power failures can be catastrophic, causing:

Blackouts affecting homes and businesses.

Voltage fluctuations damaging electrical equipment.

Overloading of transformers and substations.

A smart grid must **detect faults early** and **redistribute power intelligently** to prevent cascading failures.

How MARL Enables Smart Grid Optimization

Multi-Agent Reinforcement Learning (MARL) is well-suited for smart grid management because:

Energy suppliers, storage units, and consumers can act as independent agents that optimize local energy use while collaborating for global efficiency.

Agents continuously learn and adapt to changing demand, supply, and pricing conditions.

Distributed learning eliminates the need for a single central controller, making the system more scalable and fault-tolerant.

How MARL Works in Smart Grids

Each agent (e.g., a power plant, a solar panel, a battery storage system, or a household) learns through **reinforcement learning (RL)** by:

Observing the current grid state (demand, supply, price, etc.).

Taking an action (e.g., increasing or decreasing power production, adjusting battery charging, buying or selling electricity).

Receiving a reward based on energy efficiency, cost reduction, and grid stability.

The agent's goal is to **maximize its long-term reward**, leading to optimal grid performance.

Reward Function for Energy Agents

A reward function can be designed as:

$$R = -\alpha \cdot |P_{\text{demand}} - P_{\text{supplied}}| - \beta \cdot C_{\text{cost}} + \gamma \cdot S_{\text{stability}}$$

where:

$P_{\text{demand}} - P_{\text{supplied}}$ represents the **power balance error** (the closer to zero, the better).

C_{cost} is the **cost of electricity generation or purchase**.

$S_{\text{stability}}$ rewards maintaining **stable voltage and frequency levels**.

By optimizing this reward, MARL agents learn to **balance supply and demand efficiently** while minimizing costs.

Real-World Applications of MARL in Smart Grids

1. Demand Response Optimization

Energy companies use MARL to **adjust electricity prices in real-time** based on demand.

Consumers receive **incentives to shift usage** to off-peak hours (e.g., running dishwashers at night).

2. Dynamic Energy Storage Management

MARL agents manage **battery storage in electric vehicles (EVs)** and **grid-scale batteries**.

Agents decide **when to charge/discharge batteries** to store excess energy and release it when demand is high.

3. Peer-to-Peer (P2P) Energy Trading

Households with **solar panels** use MARL to **decide when to sell electricity** based on **market prices and demand forecasts**.

Decentralized MARL-based trading eliminates the need for **a central authority** in local energy markets.

4. Predictive Grid Maintenance and Fault Detection

MARL agents **predict potential failures** by analyzing voltage fluctuations, current loads, and past failures.

Smart grids **automatically reroute electricity** to prevent power outages.

Implementing MARL for Smart Grid Energy Management in Python

Let's implement a **basic MARL simulation** where energy producers, consumers, and storage units interact to balance supply and demand.

Step 1: Install Dependencies

```
pip install numpy tensorflow keras
```

Step 2: Define the Energy Agent

```python
import numpy as np
import tensorflow as tf
from tensorflow import keras

class EnergyAgent:
    def __init__(self, state_size, action_size):
        self.model = keras.Sequential([
            keras.layers.Dense(64,
activation='relu', input_shape=(state_size,)),
            keras.layers.Dense(64,
activation='relu'),
            keras.layers.Dense(action_size,
activation='softmax')
        ])

self.model.compile(optimizer=keras.optimizers.Adam(
learning_rate=0.001),
loss='categorical_crossentropy')
```

```python
    def select_action(self, state):
        """Chooses an action based on energy
conditions"""
        action_probabilities =
self.model.predict(np.array([state]))[0]
        return np.argmax(action_probabilities)

    def train(self, state, action, reward,
next_state):
        """Updates the policy using Q-learning"""
        target = reward + 0.9 *
np.max(self.model.predict(np.array([next_state])))[0
])
        target_vector =
self.model.predict(np.array([state]))[0]
        target_vector[action] = target
        self.model.fit(np.array([state]),
np.array([target_vector]), epochs=1, verbose=0)


# Initialize agents for energy producers,
consumers, and storage units
producers = [EnergyAgent(state_size=4,
action_size=3) for _ in range(3)]
consumers = [EnergyAgent(state_size=4,
action_size=3) for _ in range(3)]
storage_units = [EnergyAgent(state_size=4,
action_size=3) for _ in range(2)]
```

Step 3: Simulating Energy Management Decisions

```python
for episode in range(100):
    for agent in producers + consumers +
storage_units:
        state = np.random.rand(4)  # Simulated grid
state
        action = agent.select_action(state)
        reward = np.random.rand()  # Simulated
reward
        next_state = np.random.rand(4)
        agent.train(state, action, reward,
next_state)
```

```
print("Training complete. Agents can now optimize
smart grid energy distribution.")
```

This setup allows agents to **learn energy optimization strategies**, improving efficiency **without central control**.

MARL-based smart grid energy management transforms **power distribution, demand response, and renewable energy integration**. By allowing **distributed, intelligent decision-making**, MARL enables scalable, **adaptive** energy management systems that reduce costs and improve **grid stability**— paving the way for a more **efficient and sustainable energy future**.

Multi-Agent Coordination in Self-Driving Cars

Self-driving cars rely on **artificial intelligence (AI), sensors, and real-time decision-making** to navigate roads safely. However, autonomous vehicles do not operate in isolation. They must **coordinate with other vehicles, pedestrians, and traffic systems** to ensure efficient and safe transportation.

Multi-Agent Reinforcement Learning (MARL) provides a **powerful framework** for enabling self-driving cars to learn **cooperative and competitive behaviors** in traffic environments. Instead of following **static rule-based systems**, MARL allows autonomous vehicles to **adapt dynamically**, make **real-time decisions**, and improve overall traffic flow.

Why Multi-Agent Coordination is Essential for Self-Driving Cars

1. Traffic is a Multi-Agent System

Road networks involve multiple independent **decision-making entities**, including:

Self-driving cars

Human-driven vehicles

Pedestrians

165

Traffic signals and infrastructure

Each entity has its own **objectives and constraints**. Self-driving cars must:

Avoid collisions while navigating unpredictable environments.

Negotiate merging, overtaking, and lane changes with other vehicles.

Optimize routes to reduce travel time and fuel consumption.

Coordinating these objectives **efficiently and safely** is a complex problem, making **multi-agent learning** an ideal solution.

2. Traditional Traffic Coordination is Inefficient

Most traffic control systems rely on **fixed rules**, such as:

Traffic lights operating on **predefined timers**, regardless of real-time traffic conditions.

Vehicles following **static lane-changing heuristics**, which do not adapt to dynamic congestion levels.

These approaches lead to **inefficiencies, delays, and increased fuel consumption**. Self-driving cars equipped with MARL can **optimize their behaviors collectively**, improving traffic flow.

3. Safe and Efficient Merging and Overtaking

Self-driving cars often need to **merge onto highways, overtake slower vehicles, and navigate intersections**. Without coordination, vehicles may **hesitate or make conflicting decisions**, leading to congestion or accidents.

For example:

When merging onto a highway, self-driving cars must **negotiate speed adjustments** with vehicles already on the road.

If multiple cars attempt to **merge into the same lane**, MARL enables them to **predict each other's actions** and coordinate smoothly.

How MARL Enables Coordination Among Self-Driving Cars

Multi-Agent Reinforcement Learning (MARL) is a machine learning approach that allows multiple agents (self-driving cars) to learn **cooperative and competitive behaviors** through experience.

Key Components of MARL in Traffic Coordination

Agents – Each self-driving car is an agent that learns to optimize its own behavior while considering the actions of others.

State Space – The agent's perception of its environment, including:

Current speed, position, and acceleration.

Distance from nearby vehicles.

Traffic signals and road conditions.

Actions – The agent can take actions such as:

Accelerating or decelerating.

Changing lanes.

Stopping at intersections.

Rewards – The agent receives feedback based on:

Safety (avoiding collisions).

Efficiency (reducing travel time).

Energy consumption (minimizing unnecessary acceleration and braking).

Example Reward Function for a Self-Driving Car

$$R = -\alpha \cdot C_{\text{collision}} - \beta \cdot T_{\text{travel}} + \gamma \cdot E_{\text{efficiency}}$$

where:

$C_{\text{collision}}$ is a penalty for collisions.

T_{travel} is the total travel time (lower is better).

$E_{\text{efficiency}}$ rewards energy-efficient driving.

The goal of MARL is to **train self-driving cars to maximize rewards**, leading to **smooth and cooperative driving behaviors**.

Techniques for Multi-Agent Coordination in Self-Driving Cars

1. Cooperative Lane Merging

When multiple autonomous vehicles approach a highway on-ramp, they must **merge smoothly** without stopping traffic.

MARL-based cars learn to:

Adjust speed early to create space for merging cars.

Negotiate merging order through vehicle-to-vehicle communication.

Reduce unnecessary braking, preventing congestion.

2. Adaptive Traffic Signal Control

Instead of **fixed-timing traffic lights**, MARL agents **adjust signal durations dynamically** based on real-time traffic conditions.

Benefits:

Reduces **idle waiting time** at intersections.

Improves **fuel efficiency** by minimizing stop-and-go driving.

Prevents **traffic buildup** by allowing priority flow where needed.

3. Intersection Negotiation Without Traffic Lights

Self-driving cars at intersections can **self-organize** without needing traffic lights by:

Exchanging **intended paths and estimated arrival times**.

Slowing down or accelerating to avoid conflicts.

Using **collision-free trajectory optimization** to pass through intersections without stopping.

4. Platooning for Fuel Efficiency

Platooning is when a **group of self-driving cars forms a convoy**, reducing air resistance and improving fuel efficiency.

MARL-based platooning:

Optimizes following distances for minimal drag.

Coordinates acceleration and braking to maintain synchronization.

Reduces lane-changing disruptions in heavy traffic.

Real-World Applications and Case Studies

1. Waymo's Self-Driving Car Coordination

Waymo's autonomous vehicles **communicate with each other** to optimize merging, overtaking, and pedestrian safety.

The system **prioritizes cooperative driving**, reducing unnecessary braking and lane changes.

2. Tesla's Autopilot and Traffic Awareness

Tesla's AI adjusts vehicle speed dynamically based on **traffic density**.

Uses **multi-agent sensing** to avoid sudden braking or unpredictable lane changes.

3. Intelligent Highway Systems in China

MARL-based self-driving coordination is being tested for **automated toll lane merging**.

Reduces congestion and improves **entry speed consistency**.

Implementing MARL for Self-Driving Car Coordination in Python

Let's build a **simple MARL simulation** where self-driving cars learn to optimize merging behavior.

Step 1: Install Dependencies

```
pip install numpy tensorflow keras
```

Step 2: Define the Self-Driving Car Agent

```python
import numpy as np
import tensorflow as tf
from tensorflow import keras

class SelfDrivingAgent:
    def __init__(self, state_size, action_size):
        self.model = keras.Sequential([
            keras.layers.Dense(64,
activation='relu', input_shape=(state_size,)),
            keras.layers.Dense(64,
activation='relu'),
            keras.layers.Dense(action_size,
activation='softmax')
        ])

self.model.compile(optimizer=keras.optimizers.Adam(
learning_rate=0.001),
loss='categorical_crossentropy')

    def select_action(self, state):
        """Chooses an action based on traffic
conditions"""
        action_probabilities =
self.model.predict(np.array([state]))[0]
        return np.argmax(action_probabilities)

    def train(self, state, action, reward,
next_state):
        """Updates the policy using reinforcement
learning"""
        target = reward + 0.9 *
np.max(self.model.predict(np.array([next_state]))[0
])
        target_vector =
self.model.predict(np.array([state]))[0]
        target_vector[action] = target
        self.model.fit(np.array([state]),
np.array([target_vector]), epochs=1, verbose=0)

# Initialize a fleet of self-driving cars
```

```
cars = [SelfDrivingAgent(state_size=4,
action_size=3) for _ in range(5)]
```

Step 3: Simulating Traffic Coordination

```
for episode in range(100):
    for car in cars:
        state = np.random.rand(4)  # Simulated
traffic conditions
        action = car.select_action(state)
        reward = np.random.rand()  # Simulated
efficiency reward
        next_state = np.random.rand(4)
        car.train(state, action, reward,
next_state)

print("Training complete. Cars can now coordinate
merging and lane changes.")
```

MARL enables self-driving cars to **coordinate seamlessly**, reducing congestion, improving safety, and optimizing fuel efficiency. These techniques will play a crucial role in **the future of intelligent transportation systems**, making roads **safer and more efficient** for all users.

Algorithmic Trading and Financial Modeling Using MARL

Financial markets are **highly complex, dynamic, and competitive**. Traders, hedge funds, and financial institutions operate in a system where **millions of buy and sell orders are executed every second**, creating a challenging environment for decision-making. Traditional trading strategies rely on **technical indicators, statistical models, and human intuition**, but these methods struggle to adapt to **rapidly changing market conditions**.

Algorithmic trading refers to the use of **automated systems** to execute trades based on predefined rules and strategies. In recent years, **machine learning**

and **reinforcement learning** have revolutionized this field by enabling **data-driven, adaptive trading systems**.

Multi-Agent Reinforcement Learning (MARL) is particularly well-suited for financial markets because:

The market consists of **multiple competing and cooperating agents** (traders, institutions, algorithms).

The **actions of one agent affect others**, creating a dynamic and interdependent environment.

Agents must **adapt continuously** as market conditions change.

This discussion will cover:

How algorithmic trading works

How MARL enables adaptive trading strategies

Key techniques used in MARL for financial modeling

Real-world applications of MARL in finance

A practical implementation of MARL for trading strategies

How Algorithmic Trading Works

Algorithmic trading (or **algo-trading**) uses **computer programs and algorithms** to execute financial trades **automatically** based on a set of rules. These rules can be based on:

Price movements (e.g., buying when prices drop by 2% in a day).

Technical indicators (e.g., moving averages, Bollinger Bands).

Order book dynamics (e.g., market depth, bid-ask spreads).

Benefits of Algorithmic Trading

Speed – Executes trades in milliseconds, much faster than human traders.

Efficiency – Can analyze large datasets and make real-time decisions.

Emotion-Free Trading – Eliminates human biases like fear and greed.

Scalability – Can manage multiple markets and asset classes simultaneously.

However, **traditional rule-based algorithmic trading has limitations**. It struggles with:

Rapid market changes that break fixed rules.

Adapting to new market conditions without manual adjustments.

Interacting intelligently with other traders and market participants.

This is where **Multi-Agent Reinforcement Learning (MARL)** provides a significant advantage.

How MARL Enhances Algorithmic Trading

MARL treats financial markets as **a multi-agent system**, where different traders (agents) compete and cooperate to **maximize profits**. Each agent **learns to optimize its trading strategy** by interacting with the market, adjusting its actions based on **real-time feedback**.

Key Concepts in MARL for Trading

State Space – Represents market conditions, including:

Current and historical prices.

Trading volume.

Market volatility.

Economic indicators (e.g., interest rates).

Actions – Decisions that a trading agent can take, such as:

Buying or selling a financial asset.

Adjusting order sizes.

Holding positions to minimize risk.

Rewards – The agent receives feedback based on:

Profit and loss (PnL) – Maximizing returns while minimizing losses.

Risk management – Avoiding excessive exposure to volatile assets.

Execution efficiency – Reducing slippage and transaction costs.

Learning Process – The agent continuously **updates its strategy** based on market conditions and the success of past trades.

Key MARL Techniques for Financial Modeling

1. Market-Making Strategies

Market makers provide liquidity by **placing buy and sell orders** at different price levels. A MARL-based market-making agent learns to:

Optimize **bid-ask spreads** to maximize profit while maintaining liquidity.

Adjust order sizes based on **market conditions and order flow**.

Prevent losses from **adverse price movements**.

2. Momentum and Mean Reversion Trading

Momentum trading – Buying assets that are rising and selling those that are falling.

Mean reversion – Buying undervalued assets and selling overvalued ones, assuming prices revert to their mean.

MARL helps agents detect patterns and **adjust trading strategies dynamically** based on shifting trends.

3. Arbitrage and Statistical Arbitrage

Arbitrage – Exploiting price differences between markets (e.g., Bitcoin trading at different prices on two exchanges).

Statistical arbitrage – Using mathematical models to identify mispriced assets.

MARL enables agents to **execute arbitrage opportunities faster** than human traders.

4. Portfolio Optimization and Risk Management

Trading agents must **balance profit-seeking behavior with risk management**. MARL helps with:

Diversifying investments across assets.

Adjusting positions based on market volatility.

Reducing exposure to high-risk trades.

Real-World Applications of MARL in Finance

1. High-Frequency Trading (HFT)

HFT firms use MARL to:

Execute thousands of trades per second.

Detect microsecond price inefficiencies.

React instantly to market events.

2. Hedge Funds and Asset Management

Hedge funds use MARL for:

Portfolio management to balance risk and return.

Dynamic asset allocation based on market trends.

3. Market Simulation and Policy Testing

Regulators and financial institutions use MARL to:

Simulate market conditions and test trading policies.

Analyze how algorithmic traders impact financial stability.

Implementing MARL for Trading Strategies in Python

Now, let's implement a **simple MARL trading agent** that learns to optimize buy and sell decisions.

Step 1: Install Dependencies

```
pip install numpy pandas tensorflow keras gym
```

Step 2: Define the Trading Agent

```
import numpy as np
```

```python
import tensorflow as tf
from tensorflow import keras

class TradingAgent:
    def __init__(self, state_size, action_size):
        self.model = keras.Sequential([
            keras.layers.Dense(64,
activation='relu', input_shape=(state_size,)),
            keras.layers.Dense(64,
activation='relu'),
            keras.layers.Dense(action_size,
activation='softmax')
        ])

self.model.compile(optimizer=keras.optimizers.Adam(
learning_rate=0.001),
loss='categorical_crossentropy')

    def select_action(self, state):
        """Chooses an action based on market
conditions"""
        action_probabilities =
self.model.predict(np.array([state]))[0]
        return np.argmax(action_probabilities)

    def train(self, state, action, reward,
next_state):
        """Updates the policy using reinforcement
learning"""
        target = reward + 0.9 *
np.max(self.model.predict(np.array([next_state]))[0
])
        target_vector =
self.model.predict(np.array([state]))[0]
        target_vector[action] = target
        self.model.fit(np.array([state]),
np.array([target_vector]), epochs=1, verbose=0)

# Initialize trading agents for a multi-agent
simulation
agents = [TradingAgent(state_size=4, action_size=3)
for _ in range(5)]
```

Step 3: Simulating Trading Decisions

```python
for episode in range(100):
    for agent in agents:
        state = np.random.rand(4)  # Simulated
market conditions
        action = agent.select_action(state)
        reward = np.random.rand()  # Simulated
profit/loss
        next_state = np.random.rand(4)
        agent.train(state, action, reward,
next_state)

print("Training complete. Agents can now trade
based on learned strategies.")
```

Multi-Agent Reinforcement Learning (MARL) is transforming **algorithmic trading and financial modeling** by enabling **data-driven, adaptive decision-making**. These techniques are used in **hedge funds, high-frequency trading, risk management, and asset allocation**, making markets **more efficient and responsive**.

As MARL continues to evolve, it will play an even bigger role in **predicting market movements, optimizing trading strategies, and ensuring financial stability** in modern economies.

11. Challenges and Future Directions in MARL

Multi-Agent Reinforcement Learning (MARL) has advanced significantly in recent years, enabling applications in **autonomous systems, financial modeling, smart grids, and robotics**. However, despite its success, MARL faces **critical challenges** that hinder its deployment in real-world systems.

This chapter explores **four key challenges** in MARL and discusses **future research directions** to improve sample efficiency, interpretability, ethical considerations, and scalability.

Sample Efficiency and Scalability Issues in MARL

Multi-Agent Reinforcement Learning (MARL) enables intelligent systems to learn **optimal strategies** through interactions in **dynamic environments**. However, as the number of agents increases, MARL faces two significant challenges:

Sample Efficiency – The ability of an agent to learn effective policies using as few interactions as possible.

Scalability – The ability of MARL algorithms to perform well as the number of agents grows.

Both challenges **impact training speed, computational costs, and real-world applicability**. Addressing these issues is critical for deploying MARL in complex environments such as **smart traffic management, autonomous robots, financial markets, and large-scale simulations**.

Why Sample Efficiency is a Challenge in MARL

The Problem of Data-Hungry Learning

Reinforcement Learning (RL) requires **trial-and-error exploration** to learn optimal behaviors. Each agent interacts with the environment, collects experiences, and updates its policy based on rewards received. In single-agent

RL, this process already demands a large number of interactions. **In MARL, the problem is magnified** because:

Each agent's actions affect the learning process of other agents.

The environment becomes highly dynamic, making it harder to generalize from past experiences.

Exploration becomes inefficient because agents must not only learn their own behaviors but also predict how others will behave.

For example, in **autonomous traffic control**, an intelligent traffic light must adjust signal timings while considering:

The movement of vehicles at the intersection.

The strategies of nearby intersections.

Fluctuations in real-time traffic flow.

If the system learns too slowly, **traffic congestion worsens before optimal policies are found**.

Inefficient Exploration in MARL

Exploration refers to the process of trying different actions to discover which ones yield the highest rewards. In MARL:

Naive exploration leads to redundant learning, where multiple agents repeatedly test the same suboptimal actions.

Agents may interfere with each other's learning, causing unstable policies.

Sparse rewards slow down progress, making it difficult for agents to identify good strategies.

For example, in a **multi-drone delivery system**, drones must explore:

Different delivery routes.

Efficient flight paths.

Collision avoidance strategies.

If each drone **explores independently without coordination**, learning efficiency is reduced, leading to **delays in training and real-world deployment**.

Why MARL Struggles with Scalability

The Curse of Dimensionality in Large Agent Systems

As the number of agents increases, the **state-action space grows exponentially**. This is known as the **curse of dimensionality**, making MARL systems:

Slower to train, as each agent must account for more variables.

Harder to optimize, since policies must adapt to a wider range of interactions.

More memory-intensive, requiring massive computational resources.

For example, in **large-scale swarm robotics**, thousands of robots must coordinate without explicit centralized control. As the number of agents grows, the complexity of **learning effective group behaviors increases significantly**.

Non-Stationarity in MARL

In a multi-agent environment, the learning process is **constantly changing** because each agent **updates its policy over time**. This creates a **non-stationary environment**, making it difficult for agents to:

Predict future outcomes based on past experiences.

Learn stable strategies since **other agents keep changing their behaviors**.

Generalize across different scenarios, requiring continuous retraining.

For example, in **multi-agent financial trading**, if one trading bot adjusts its strategy, it alters market conditions for all other bots, making previously learned policies less effective.

Techniques to Improve Sample Efficiency and Scalability

1. Experience Replay with Shared Memory

Experience replay stores past interactions and reuses them for training, reducing the need for new data collection. In MARL, **shared experience replay** enables agents to learn from **each other's experiences**, improving sample efficiency.

How it helps:

Reduces redundant exploration.

Accelerates learning by leveraging experiences from multiple agents.

Improves convergence to optimal policies.

Example: In **autonomous warehouse robots,** if one robot learns to avoid a congested aisle, **other robots can reuse that experience** instead of rediscovering the same rule.

2. Parameter Sharing Across Agents

Instead of training separate models for each agent, **parameter sharing** allows multiple agents to share a single neural network. This approach:

Reduces computational costs.

Improves learning efficiency by leveraging **shared representations**.

Helps generalize across different agent behaviors.

Example: In **multi-agent drone navigation,** all drones can **use a common policy network,** ensuring efficient learning across different flight paths.

3. Curriculum Learning for Progressive Complexity

Curriculum learning introduces simpler tasks before progressing to complex ones. In MARL, agents first **learn basic coordination** before tackling **full-scale multi-agent environments**.

How it helps:

Prevents agents from being overwhelmed by complex interactions.

Encourages **faster convergence** by starting with structured learning tasks.

Example: In **robotic soccer**, agents first learn to **pass the ball** before being trained on full-team coordination.

4. Graph Neural Networks (GNNs) for Multi-Agent Interactions

GNNs allow MARL models to process **structured multi-agent interactions**, making them more scalable. Instead of treating all agents as separate entities, GNNs:

Represent agents as **nodes** in a graph.

Learn relationships between agents based on **neighboring interactions**.

Reduce the computational cost of modeling **large agent groups**.

Example: In **swarm robotics**, GNN-based MARL enables robots to **coordinate efficiently**, regardless of the swarm size.

5. Centralized Training with Decentralized Execution (CTDE)

CTDE trains agents using a **centralized model** while allowing each agent to make decisions **independently during execution**.

How it helps:

Efficient training using global knowledge.

Decentralized execution, making agents adaptable in real-world settings.

Scalability, allowing MARL systems to handle **large agent populations**.

Example: In **smart grid energy management**, power stations **learn optimal energy distribution centrally** but execute policies **locally** based on real-time demand.

Real-World Applications Where These Improvements Are Crucial

1. Large-Scale Autonomous Traffic Systems

Traffic signals and self-driving cars coordinate to minimize congestion.

CTDE improves real-time decision-making, balancing efficiency and safety.

2. Financial Markets and Trading Bots

MARL-based trading systems **scale across global markets**.

Experience replay allows traders to **learn from historical patterns**, improving **sample efficiency**.

3. Multi-Robot Industrial Automation

In **Amazon's warehouse robotics**, parameter sharing helps robots efficiently **optimize storage and retrieval tasks**.

GNN-based MARL enables coordination among thousands of robots **without direct communication overhead**.

4. Military and Defense Simulations

Large-scale MARL simulations improve **strategic planning** in multi-agent warfare.

Curriculum learning ensures progressive training, **optimizing coordination at scale**.

MARL holds immense potential for **real-world autonomous systems**, but challenges in **sample efficiency and scalability** must be addressed for broader adoption. By leveraging techniques such as **experience replay, parameter sharing, GNNs, and curriculum learning**, MARL models can train faster, generalize better, and operate effectively **in large-scale environments**.

As research progresses, MARL will play a critical role in **intelligent transportation, finance, industrial automation, and large-scale robotics**, transforming the way autonomous systems learn and interact.

Trust and Interpretability in MARL Systems

Multi-Agent Reinforcement Learning (MARL) enables intelligent agents to interact, learn, and make autonomous decisions in complex environments. While MARL has been successful in applications such as **autonomous vehicles, financial trading, smart grids, and robotic coordination**, a major challenge remains: **trust and interpretability**.

For MARL to be deployed in **high-stakes environments**—such as healthcare, finance, or defense—users must understand and trust the decisions made by AI agents. However, MARL systems are often treated as **black boxes**, meaning their decision-making processes are **difficult to interpret**.

Why Trust and Interpretability Matter in MARL

1. Decision Transparency in High-Stakes Applications

Many MARL applications require **clear explanations** for decisions, especially in **safety-critical environments**.

For example:

In **autonomous driving**, self-driving cars must explain **why** they take specific actions in traffic.

In **financial trading**, AI-powered trading bots must justify **investment decisions** to avoid regulatory violations.

In **healthcare AI**, MARL systems assisting in **surgical robotics or drug discovery** must provide understandable insights to medical professionals.

If humans cannot **understand** why MARL agents make certain choices, they will be reluctant to **trust or adopt** these systems.

2. Debugging and Error Detection

Without interpretability, **detecting errors in MARL policies is difficult**.

A MARL system may develop **unintended behaviors** that lead to inefficiencies or risks.

Engineers and researchers need **transparent models** to identify and fix **unexpected agent behaviors**.

For example, in **multi-agent drone coordination**, if drones start **colliding or taking inefficient paths**, developers need tools to **trace the decision-making process** and correct faulty logic.

3. Ethical and Regulatory Compliance

In areas such as **finance, healthcare, and defense**, AI systems must meet **ethical guidelines and regulatory standards**.

Regulators require explanations for automated decisions in trading and lending.

Medical professionals must trust AI recommendations before integrating them into patient care.

Military and defense AI systems must be accountable, ensuring compliance with legal and ethical standards.

If MARL models operate **without transparency**, they **risk violating regulations** and may be **banned from critical applications**.

Challenges in Making MARL Systems Interpretable

1. Complexity of Multi-Agent Interactions

Unlike **single-agent reinforcement learning**, where one agent learns in a controlled environment, MARL involves **multiple agents learning simultaneously**. This creates challenges such as:

Dynamic environments where agents continuously adapt to each other's behavior.

Non-stationarity, meaning past experiences may no longer apply as agents evolve.

Inter-agent dependencies, where one agent's actions impact the decisions of others, making causal relationships harder to track.

2. Deep Learning Black-Box Problem

Many MARL systems use **deep neural networks** to approximate policies. While powerful, deep networks:

Lack **transparent reasoning**—they make predictions based on learned weights without explicit rules.

Are **hard to analyze**, as millions of parameters influence decisions.

Can **overfit to patterns** that are difficult to interpret.

3. Trade-Off Between Performance and Interpretability

More interpretable models (such as rule-based systems) tend to perform worse in complex environments.

High-performance deep learning models sacrifice transparency for better accuracy.

Balancing interpretability and effectiveness is a key challenge in MARL research.

Techniques for Improving Trust and Interpretability in MARL

1. Explainable Reinforcement Learning (XRL)

XRL techniques aim to **make reinforcement learning policies easier to understand** by providing **human-readable insights** into agent decision-making.

Feature Attribution Methods

Identifies which features **most influence an agent's decision**.

Example: In **self-driving MARL**, an agent's braking decision could be attributed to **speed, distance to the car ahead, and traffic signals**.

Saliency Maps

Highlights **which parts of an input** contributed most to an agent's action.

Used in **vision-based MARL**, such as multi-agent drone navigation, to show **which objects in an image the agent is reacting to**.

2. Causal Learning in MARL

Instead of learning only from **statistical correlations**, causal learning allows MARL agents to:

Understand **cause-and-effect relationships**.

Reduce biases by **differentiating between meaningful signals and noise**.

For example, in **multi-agent financial trading**, causal learning helps:

Distinguish between **market fluctuations and genuine long-term trends**.

Avoid incorrect strategies based on **short-term correlations**.

3. Policy Visualization and Rule Extraction

One approach to improving interpretability is **converting MARL policies into human-readable rules**.

Decision Tree Approximation

Converts deep learning-based MARL policies into **decision trees**.

Example: In **multi-agent healthcare AI**, a decision tree can outline **treatment steps chosen by AI-assisted doctors**.

Graph-Based Interpretability

Uses **graph neural networks (GNNs)** to represent relationships between MARL agents.

Example: In **traffic coordination**, a GNN could visualize how self-driving cars **communicate and adjust their routes dynamically**.

4. Human-in-the-Loop MARL

Instead of fully autonomous systems, **human oversight and feedback** can improve MARL interpretability.

Interactive Policy Learning: Humans provide feedback on AI-generated decisions, helping agents adjust strategies.

Confidence Scores: Agents assign a confidence level to their actions, making it clear **when decisions are uncertain**.

For example, in **AI-assisted air traffic control**, human experts monitor AI recommendations and intervene when necessary.

Real-World Applications Where Interpretability is Crucial

1. Autonomous Vehicles

MARL helps **self-driving fleets coordinate**, but **interpretable policies** ensure humans understand how decisions are made.

Transparency prevents **legal issues in case of accidents**.

2. Algorithmic Trading and Finance

Regulatory agencies require financial AI models to be **explainable**.

Transparent MARL models prevent **black-box trading strategies** that could cause financial instability.

3. Healthcare AI

AI-driven **drug discovery and patient diagnosis** must be interpretable so that **doctors and researchers can validate results**.

Lack of transparency can **lead to incorrect treatments** or **legal consequences**.

4. Multi-Agent Cybersecurity

AI systems managing **cyber defense must explain why certain threats are flagged**.

Interpretability ensures **trust in automated security decisions**.

For MARL to gain widespread adoption in **autonomous systems, finance, healthcare, and security**, it must become more **interpretable and trustworthy**. Researchers and developers are working on:

Explainable reinforcement learning to provide human-readable insights.

Causal learning to differentiate between meaningful trends and random noise.

Human-in-the-loop models to integrate AI decisions with human oversight.

By improving interpretability, MARL will not only become **more transparent and reliable** but also **more widely accepted in real-world applications** where accountability is crucial.

Ethical Considerations in Competitive AI Agents

Artificial Intelligence (AI) agents are increasingly being used in **competitive environments** such as **financial markets, strategic gaming, cybersecurity, and automated negotiations**. While competition can drive innovation and efficiency, it also introduces **ethical concerns** related to fairness, accountability, bias, and unintended consequences.

When multiple AI agents compete for resources, information, or dominance, there is potential for:

Unfair advantages and collusion—AI systems manipulating markets or decision-making processes.

Deceptive strategies—Agents learning to exploit loopholes rather than engaging in fair competition.

Social and economic inequalities—Reinforcement learning models amplifying biases in finance, hiring, or law enforcement.

Ethical Risks of Competitive AI Agents

1. Unfair Competitive Behavior and Collusion

Competitive AI agents aim to maximize their rewards, but without ethical constraints, they may **learn to manipulate systems for unfair advantage**.

For example, in **financial trading**, reinforcement learning models may:

Engage in price manipulation, artificially inflating or deflating stock prices.

Learn to coordinate trades (collusion), unfairly influencing market trends.

Exploit latency advantages, executing trades faster than human traders in ways that harm market fairness.

Example Case: Flash Crash of 2010
In 2010, **high-frequency trading (HFT) algorithms** contributed to a market crash, where stock prices fluctuated wildly in minutes due to **automated decision loops** reacting unpredictably.

189

2. Deception and Exploitative Strategies

AI agents trained in **competitive reinforcement learning** may discover deceptive behaviors that maximize rewards while **breaking ethical norms**.

For example, in **automated negotiations**:

AI may **misrepresent information** to gain leverage.

Strategic delay tactics may be used to wear down opponents.

In **cybersecurity**, AI systems designed for **defensive measures** can also be **repurposed for offensive attacks**, escalating AI-driven cyber warfare.

3. Reinforcement of Bias and Social Inequality

When competitive AI agents operate in domains like **hiring, lending, or law enforcement**, they can:

Learn **biased decision-making patterns** from historical data.

Prioritize profit over fairness, discriminating against underrepresented groups.

Example: Bias in Hiring Algorithms
A recruitment AI that **competes for the best candidates** may:

Favor applicants **from privileged backgrounds** based on historical hiring data.

Penalize candidates who **don't fit previous patterns**, reducing diversity.

4. Ethical Challenges in Autonomous Weapons and AI Warfare

Military AI systems trained for **defense strategies** may:

Learn to **neutralize threats preemptively**, raising concerns about **autonomous decision-making in life-or-death scenarios**.

Optimize for **combat effectiveness**, ignoring humanitarian considerations.

Governments and organizations are debating whether **AI-driven autonomous weapons** should ever be allowed to **make lethal decisions without human intervention**.

Real-World Applications and Ethical Concerns

1. AI in High-Frequency Trading (HFT)

AI-powered trading bots engage in **microsecond trading battles** to maximize profits.

Ethical concern: Lack of transparency can lead to **market instability and crashes**.

2. AI in Competitive E-Sports and Games

AI agents trained in **strategic games (e.g., Dota 2, StarCraft)** learn to **outsmart human players**.

Ethical concern: AI dominance in competitive gaming raises **questions about fair play and accessibility**.

3. AI in Job Market and Recruitment

AI competing for **top candidates** may prioritize efficiency over **fairness and diversity**.

Ethical concern: Bias in AI hiring could **reduce opportunities for underrepresented groups**.

4. AI in Automated Negotiations

Companies use AI to **optimize negotiations** in contracts, pricing, and mergers.

Ethical concern: AI may learn to **exploit cognitive biases**, leading to **unethical business practices**.

Strategies for Ensuring Ethical AI Behavior

1. Ethical Reward Design in MARL

Reinforcement learning agents maximize rewards. **Ethical AI design ensures that rewards align with human values**.

Solution: Multi-Objective Reward Functions

Instead of rewarding only profit or efficiency, AI can be trained with:

$$R_{\text{total}} = R_{\text{performance}} - \lambda R_{\text{unethical\_behavior}}$$

where:

$R_{\text{performance}}$ measures success in the task.

$R_{\text{unethical\_behavior}}$ penalizes deceptive or harmful strategies.

For example, in **automated trading**, a reward function could:

Reward stable, fair trading.

Penalize manipulative or deceptive practices.

2. Human Oversight and AI Accountability

Competitive AI should not operate without **human supervision**. Organizations should implement:

Audit trails, ensuring AI decisions can be reviewed.

AI transparency policies, explaining how decisions are made.

Kill switches, allowing humans to override harmful AI actions.

For example, in **cybersecurity**, AI-driven threat detection should allow **human review** before taking critical actions like **blocking entire networks**.

3. AI Ethics Regulations and Global Standards

Governments and institutions are developing **ethical guidelines for AI competition**. Some key initiatives include:

EU AI Act – Regulating high-risk AI applications.

IEEE Ethically Aligned Design – Defining AI fairness standards.

UN AI for Good – Encouraging responsible AI development globally.

Companies developing **autonomous trading, AI warfare, and competitive AI models** must comply with emerging **global regulations** to ensure fair and safe AI deployment.

Competitive AI agents **offer immense benefits**, but they also introduce serious **ethical risks**. To ensure **fair, transparent, and accountable AI systems**, developers must:

Design ethical reward functions that discourage harmful behaviors.

Implement human oversight to prevent AI misuse.

Comply with global AI ethics regulations to ensure responsible deployment.

As AI continues to evolve, balancing **competition, ethics, and accountability** will be **essential** for creating AI systems that benefit society while minimizing risks.

Future Trends in Multi-Agent AI

Multi-Agent Artificial Intelligence (Multi-Agent AI) is rapidly evolving, with applications ranging from **autonomous vehicles and smart grids to financial markets and robotics**. As AI systems become more interconnected, the ability of multiple AI agents to **learn, cooperate, and compete effectively** is becoming increasingly important.

The future of Multi-Agent AI is shaped by advances in **machine learning, communication protocols, decentralized decision-making, and real-world applications**. This discussion explores the most significant trends that will drive the **next generation of Multi-Agent AI systems**.

1. Large-Scale Multi-Agent Learning

Current Multi-Agent AI systems typically handle **dozens to hundreds** of agents. However, real-world applications, such as **smart cities and decentralized finance**, require AI to manage **thousands or even millions** of agents simultaneously.

Future Advances

Scalable Architectures – New models will be designed to efficiently manage large numbers of agents while minimizing computational overhead.

Distributed Training Methods – Cloud and edge computing will enable decentralized training, reducing bottlenecks.

Graph Neural Networks (GNNs) – These models will allow AI to **represent and analyze relationships** between large numbers of agents efficiently.

Real-World Impact

Smart Traffic Systems will manage thousands of self-driving cars in real time.

Decentralized AI for financial markets will optimize global trading strategies without central control.

2. Multi-Agent AI in the Metaverse and Digital Environments

The **Metaverse** and digital twin simulations require AI agents to **interact naturally with humans and other AI systems** in virtual worlds.

Future Advances

AI Avatars and Digital Assistants – Agents will adapt to human behavior in virtual environments.

Persistent Multi-Agent Learning – AI will **retain and evolve** its learning across multiple virtual interactions.

AI-Powered Governance Systems – AI agents will **moderate, enforce rules, and manage economies** in digital spaces.

Real-World Impact

AI-driven virtual economies will manage digital transactions in real time.

Multi-Agent AI will facilitate large-scale gaming, social interactions, and e-commerce in the Metaverse.

3. Human-AI Collaboration and Teamwork

Future AI systems will not just replace human roles; they will **work alongside humans** in areas such as healthcare, engineering, and creative industries.

Future Advances

Human-in-the-Loop AI – AI agents will assist decision-making while **allowing human oversight**.

Adaptive AI Assistants – AI will learn from human preferences and adjust to different collaboration styles.

Explainable Multi-Agent AI – AI models will provide **clear reasoning** behind decisions to build trust.

Real-World Impact

AI copilots in aviation and autonomous driving will assist human operators in decision-making.

AI-assisted surgery will enable collaborative procedures between AI and human surgeons.

AI-enhanced creativity will help artists, musicians, and writers generate new ideas collaboratively.

4. Self-Learning and Self-Adapting AI Ecosystems

Most AI systems today require extensive **pretraining and human supervision**. In the future, AI agents will **self-learn, self-organize, and evolve** without direct human intervention.

Future Advances

Meta-Learning – AI will learn **how to learn**, allowing faster adaptation to new environments.

Continual Learning – AI agents will retain knowledge and **adapt over time** instead of resetting with every new task.

Autonomous Goal Formation – AI systems will **generate their own learning objectives** based on environmental feedback.

Real-World Impact

Self-learning robots will improve efficiency in logistics and manufacturing.

Financial AI agents will dynamically adjust investment strategies without retraining.

AI-driven smart cities will continuously optimize energy use, traffic, and public services.

5. Multi-Agent AI in Cybersecurity and Defense

Cyber threats are becoming more **automated and adaptive**, requiring AI-powered security systems that can **detect and respond to attacks in real time**.

Future Advances

AI vs. AI Cybersecurity – Defensive AI will learn to **counteract adversarial AI attacks** in real time.

Multi-Agent Threat Intelligence – AI agents will work together to **identify and neutralize cyber threats** across multiple networks.

Decentralized Security Models – AI will manage security in **autonomous systems and IoT devices**.

Real-World Impact

AI-driven security for smart homes and IoT devices will detect cyberattacks before they happen.

Military AI systems will use multi-agent coordination for autonomous threat detection.

6. Multi-Agent AI in Decentralized Finance (DeFi) and Smart Contracts

Blockchain and **decentralized finance (DeFi)** rely on AI for **automated trading, fraud detection, and contract execution**.

Future Advances

AI-driven smart contracts – Self-learning AI models will **optimize financial agreements** dynamically.

Decentralized AI Markets – AI agents will **trade digital assets and services autonomously**.

Fraud Detection and Compliance – AI will identify **suspicious financial activities** in real time.

Real-World Impact

AI-powered crypto trading bots will autonomously optimize investments.

AI-enhanced financial audits will improve transparency in decentralized transactions.

7. Quantum Computing and Multi-Agent AI

Traditional computers struggle with large-scale **multi-agent coordination**, but **quantum computing** has the potential to **significantly accelerate AI learning**.

Future Advances

Quantum Reinforcement Learning (QRL) – AI models will use quantum computing to **solve multi-agent problems exponentially faster**.

Quantum Cryptography in Multi-Agent AI – Secure AI-based communications will become unbreakable using quantum encryption.

Quantum-Accelerated Optimization – AI will solve complex logistics, scheduling, and game-theory problems more efficiently.

Real-World Impact

Quantum-enhanced supply chain AI will optimize global logistics networks.

Quantum-powered AI traffic management will reduce urban congestion.

8. AI Ethics and Governance in Multi-Agent Systems

As AI systems become **more autonomous and influential**, ethical concerns will shape how they interact with society.

Future Advances

Regulatory AI Compliance – AI will automatically **self-audit** to ensure fairness and transparency.

AI Alignment with Human Values – Models will be trained to align with **human rights, safety, and ethical standards**.

Bias-Reduction in Multi-Agent AI – AI models will detect and **eliminate discriminatory behaviors** in decision-making.

Real-World Impact

AI ethics laws will govern how autonomous systems interact with humans.

AI-driven legal systems will improve fairness in regulatory enforcement.

The future of Multi-Agent AI is defined by **scalability, adaptability, security, and ethical AI governance**. As AI becomes **more integrated into daily life**, new technologies will drive:

Smarter autonomous vehicles optimizing real-time traffic coordination.

AI-powered financial markets managing decentralized trading systems.

Ethical AI ecosystems ensuring transparency and fairness in decision-making.

These trends will shape how AI collaborates with humans and other AI agents, leading to a future where **intelligent systems operate efficiently, ethically, and autonomously across industries**.

www.ingramcontent.com/pod-product-compliance
Lightning Source LLC
LaVergne TN
LVHW080116070326
832902LV00015B/2614